T0311396

An Analysis of

Alexis de Tocqueville's

Democracy in America

Elizabeth Morrow

www.macat.com
info@macat.com

Cover illustration: Capucine Deslouis

Cataloguing in Publication Data
A catalogue record for this book is available from the British Library.
Library of Congress Cataloguing-in-Publication Data is available upon request.

ISBN 978-1-912303-24-3 (hardback)
ISBN 978-1-912127-54-2 (paperback)
ISBN 978-1-912282-12-8 (e-book)

Notice
The information in this book is designed to orientate readers of the work under analysis,
to elucidate and contextualise its key ideas and themes, and to aid in the development
of critical thinking skills. It is not meant to be used, nor should it be used, as a
substitute for original thinking or in place of original writing or research. References and
notes are provided for informational purposes and their presence does not constitute
endorsement of the information or opinions therein. This book is presented solely for
educational purposes. It is sold on the understanding that the publisher is not engaged
to provide any scholarly advice. The publisher has made every effort to ensure that
this book is accurate and up-to-date, but makes no warranties or representations with
regard to the completeness or reliability of the information it contains. The information
and the opinions provided herein are not guaranteed or warranted to produce particular
results and may not be suitable for students of every ability. The publisher shall not be
liable for any loss, damage or disruption arising from any errors or omissions, or from
the use of this book, including, but not limited to, special, incidental, consequential or
other damages caused, or alleged to have been caused, directly or indirectly, by the
information contained within.

CONTENTS

THE MACAT LIBRARY
The Macat Library is a series of unique academic explorations of seminal works in the humanities and social sciences – books and papers that have had a significant and widely recognised impact on their disciplines. It has been created to serve as much more than just a summary of what lies between the covers of a great book. It illuminates and explores the influences on, ideas of, and impact of that book. Our goal is to offer a learning resource that encourages critical thinking and fosters a better, deeper understanding of important ideas.

Each publication is divided into three Sections: Influences, Ideas, and Impact. Each Section has four Modules. These explore every important facet of the work, and the responses to it.

This Section-Module structure makes a Macat Library book easy to use, but it has another important feature. Because each Macat book is written to the same format, it is possible (and encouraged!) to cross-reference multiple Macat books along the same lines of inquiry or research. This allows the reader to open up interesting interdisciplinary pathways.

To further aid your reading, lists of glossary terms and people mentioned are included at the end of this book (these are indicated by an asterisk [*] throughout) – as well as a list of works cited.

Macat has worked with the University of Cambridge to identify the elements of critical thinking and understand the ways in which six different skills combine to enable effective thinking.
Three allow us to fully understand a problem; three more give us the tools to solve it. Together, these six skills make up the **PACIER** model of critical thinking. They are:

ANALYSIS – understanding how an argument is built
EVALUATION – exploring the strengths and weaknesses of an argument
INTERPRETATION – understanding issues of meaning

CREATIVE THINKING – coming up with new ideas and fresh connections
PROBLEM-SOLVING – producing strong solutions
REASONING – creating strong arguments

To find out more, visit **WWW.MACAT.COM.**

CRITICAL THINKING AND DEMOCRACY IN AMERICA

Primary critical thinking skill: PROBLEM-SOLVING
Secondary critical thinking skill: REASONING

Alexis de Tocqueville's 1838 *Democracy in America* is a classic of political theory – and of the problem-solving skills central to putting forward political ideas.

Problem-solving has several aspects: identifying problems, finding methodologies to deal with them, and applying the right criteria to work out how to solve them. Indeed, offering solutions is only the last stage in a developed process of problem solving. For Tocqueville, the problem at hand was how best to run a democratic state. In the early 19th century, it seemed clear that Europe was headed in the direction of democracy, but in the wake of the French Revolution, it was unclear how to avoid the many pitfalls on that road.

Tocqueville therefore turned to America, then point the most established democracy in the world, to investigate the institutions that allowed it to run as a successful state – allowing people their say while preventing both the possible "tyranny of the majority" and the uncontrolled growth of government. Tocqueville's careful analysis of the strengths of American democracy was then applied to the problems of instituting democracy in France, providing a range of solutions that proved deeply influential in European political thought.

ABOUT THE AUTHOR OF THE ORIGINAL WORK

Alexis de Tocqueville was born into an aristocratic French family in 1805. Trained as a lawyer, he nonetheless dreamed of a political career. His belief that post-revolutionary France would eventually adopt democratic rule led to a fact-finding mission to America in 1831. Tocqueville wanted to witness first-hand how America had created a healthy democracy, hoping his findings would help his home country to embrace democracy as effectively. Tocqueville returned to hold a number of government positions in France, but died of tuberculosis in 1859 aged just 53.

ABOUT THE AUTHORS OF THE ANALYSIS

Dr Elizabeth Morrow is currently a research fellow at the Department of Political Science and International Studies, University of Birmingham. She began her career as a lawyer with the Victorian state government in Melbourne before completing her PhD in Politics in the Department of Political Economy at King's College London.

ABOUT MACAT

GREAT WORKS FOR CRITICAL THINKING

Macat is focused on making the ideas of the world's great thinkers accessible and comprehensible to everybody, everywhere, in ways that promote the development of enhanced critical thinking skills.

It works with leading academics from the world's top universities to produce new analyses that focus on the ideas and the impact of the most influential works ever written across a wide variety of academic disciplines. Each of the works that sit at the heart of its growing library is an enduring example of great thinking. But by setting them in context – and looking at the influences that shaped their authors, as well as the responses they provoked – Macat encourages readers to look at these classics and game-changers with fresh eyes. Readers learn to think, engage and challenge their ideas, rather than simply accepting them.

'Macat offers an amazing first-of-its-kind tool for
interdisciplinary learning and research. Its focus on works
that transformed their disciplines and its rigorous approach,
drawing on the world's leading experts and educational institutions,
opens up a world-class education to anyone.'

Andreas Schleicher,
Director for Education and Skills, Organisation for Economic
Co-operation and Development

'Macat is taking on some of the major challenges in university
education ... They have drawn together a strong team of active
academics who are producing teaching materials that are
novel in the breadth of their approach.'

Prof Lord Broers,
former Vice-Chancellor of the University of Cambridge

'The Macat vision is exceptionally exciting. It focuses
upon new modes of learning which analyse and explain seminal texts
which have profoundly influenced world thinking and so social and
economic development. It promotes the kind of critical thinking
which is essential for any society and economy.
This is the learning of the future.'

Rt Hon Charles Clarke, former UK Secretary of State for Education

'The Macat analyses provide immediate access to the critical
conversation surrounding the books that have shaped their
respective discipline, which will make them an invaluable resource
to all of those, students and teachers, working in the field.'

Professor William Tronzo, University of California at San Diego

WAYS IN TO THE TEXT

KEY POINTS

- Alexis de Tocqueville was a French historian and political thinker. He was born in Paris in 1805 and died in the French city of Cannes in April 1859, aged 53.

- His seminal work *Democracy in America* described the United States of America in the 1830s. The book attempted to explain America's success in introducing a democratic* form of government.

- *Democracy In America* introduced a new way of thinking about democracy in Europe by showing that democracies really could work.

Who was Alexis de Tocqueville?

Alexis de Tocqueville was born in Paris in 1805, the third son of an aristocratic French couple. His parents lived through the French Revolution* of 1789, a time of great social upheaval, and remained loyal to the royal family that had occupied the French throne since the sixteenth century—the Bourbons.*

The year before Tocqueville's birth, the military leader Napoleon Bonaparte* had been crowned Emperor of France following several years spent consolidating his power. Although he was deposed in 1814 and the Bourbons restored to the throne, by the time Tocqueville was in his mid 20s, opinion in France was again turning against the monarchy.

Sensing a shift in the political climate, and convinced that France would abandon its monarchy and become a democracy, Tocqueville became interested in the United States of America. The nation was the world's first modern democracy following the declaration of independence of 13 of Great Britain's North American colonies in 1776; two years later, it had become an ally of France on the signing of a treaty in 1778.

Tocqueville decided to study the American system at first hand, wanting to understand how the Americans had made their democracy work. By doing so, he hoped to help the French introduce democracy successfully. He also hoped that his knowledge of America would give him political clout in France. It should be noted that, although Tocqueville had trained as a lawyer, his ambition was to become a politician.

Together with his friend Gustave de Beaumont,* Tocqueville set sail for the United States in 1831 to spend nine months traveling. He published the first volume of *Democracy in America* in 1835; the second volume followed five years later. Filled with observations about the American political system and American values, the work was an immediate success.

Tocqueville went on to a career as a politician and historian. He died in 1859 at the age of just 53, but his book is still regarded as a classic text today. And his ideas still stimulate political debate, particularly in America, where his influence has been most noticeable and lasting.

What Does *Democracy in America* Say?

The question at the heart of Tocqueville's work is: "Why has democracy been successful in America?" The French had tried to introduce a democracy themselves after the Revolution of 1789. Although this attempt had proved unsuccessful, Tocqueville believed the French still wanted to live in a democracy, and his aim was to learn from America and take those lessons back to France. So as well as studying the

American political system, Tocqueville also made sure he studied American society, American values, and American institutions, thinking that all these different elements must play a role in keeping democracy healthy.

Tocqueville was aware that there were potential dangers in adopting democracy as a system of government. One particular risk he identified was that a democracy might result in an all-powerful, centralized state; the term he coined to describe it was "democratic despotism."*

He thought that a despotic democracy would be kind towards its citizens, and would have their welfare at heart but that, ultimately, it would damage them by preventing them from exercising individual effort and individual thought. If the state became too powerful, he reasoned, the people might become dependent on it. If people were too dependent on the state, they might lose the ability to think for themselves. And if people did not think for themselves, civilization itself might be threatened.

Tocqueville also noted another—related—danger in democratic rule. Democracies could potentially develop where there would be no room for minority opinions. He called this the tyranny of the majority.* If minority opinion could not be expressed and debated, then all citizens would conform and think in the same way, which would lead to stagnation and decline.

In *Democracy in America* Tocqueville discusses these problems and, especially, what the Americans had done to avoid them. He argues that the American legal system acted as an effective brake on excessive state power. More, the nation's political structures helped to prevent power from becoming overly centralized, since the decisions taken by the central government had to be carried out by authorities who operated at local level.

Local societies played an important role in a working democracy, Tocqueville noted. Americans from all walks of life and of all ages regularly came together to form groups—something that did not happen in the Europe of the 1830s. These groups could have any aim or reason for coming together at all. They could meet for religious, sporting, or philanthropic (that is, charitable or humanitarian) reasons, or simply for enjoyment; it did not matter. For Tocqueville, what was key was the fact that individuals chose to form groups in the spirit of sharing and involvement. He felt that these groups helped to keep state power under control. The fact that they existed showed that individual initiative was alive and well. They were not formed because the state had decided they should be but, rather, because individuals had decided to form them.

To Tocqueville, that showed a resilient and resourceful society rather than an unthinking, conformist one. And a society that formed groups to pursue certain goals could easily create its own forums where minority opinions could be heard. As part of a group, those opinions would have more weight and would be heard more widely. Tocqueville believed that this kind of social activity would greatly benefit Europe.

Why Does *Democracy in America* Matter?

When the first volume of *Democracy In America* was published in 1835, it introduced a new way of thinking about democracy. Although some authors before Tocqueville had argued that democracy was dangerous, that was not because they thought it would lead to conformity and minority views being heard less. On the contrary, they worried that democracy would lead to anarchy,* with nobody recognizing authority.

Tocqueville made his readers think differently. He showed that democracies really could work. He suggested that countries across Europe were already moving towards a democratic system and argued that creating a system of checks and balances to state control would make democracy healthier.

Although democratic government is tried and tested today,

Tocqueville's ideas are still relevant. In America, thinkers on both ends of the political spectrum respond to his concept of democratic despotism. Thinkers on the right believe democratic despotism would be created by expanding the welfare state,* a system where the government plays a large role in the protection of the economic and social status of its citizens. They argue that when the government provides too much protection, then it creates dependent citizens. Thinkers on the left, meanwhile, believe that it is potentially dangerous for power to become overly centralized, since this might lead a government to feel itself capable of operating independently of the law.

Tocqueville's ideas about the importance of social clubs and societies also inform current political debates. Some academics, having researched group membership, have concluded that these societies benefit both individuals and the political system. The fact that other academics disagree suggests that Tocqueville's ideas continue to stimulate debate and research. They both continue to challenge the reader to think about the way power is distributed in different political systems and encourage readers to think about how systems of government are maintained.

If Tocqueville's observations about America remain fascinating for readers today it is, in part, because he made so many accurate predictions about America's future.

He predicted that America and Russia would end up as superpowers. He predicted that they would have opposing political systems. He predicted that slavery would threaten the future of the Union (although he believed that the battle would be between the black and white populations of the South, whereas it turned out to be between the northern and southern states). And he predicted that the indigenous peoples of America would come close to destruction.

Tocqueville's foresight in all of these matters enhanced his reputation. But even without this impressive understanding, *Democracy in America* is still a fascinating read. It provides a wealth of information about America in the early 1830s and, many people believe, continues to reveal truths about America and its citizens today.

SECTION 1
INFLUENCES

MODULE 1
THE AUTHOR AND THE HISTORICAL CONTEXT

KEY POINTS

- *Democracy in America* challenged contemporary understandings of democracy.* It is still used to inform debates about the role government should play in the lives of its citizens.

- Frenchman Alexis de Tocqueville believed France was moving towards democracy and that lessons from the American experience of this form of government would be useful as it made the transition.

- Tocqueville hoped that knowledge of the United States might help him progress in his own political career.

Why Read this Text?

The two volumes of Alexis de Tocqueville's Democracy in America contain an extraordinary breadth of observations about the United States.

Tocqueville spent nine months traveling across the country between May 1831 and February 1832, gathering information on subjects as diverse as racial inequality and the dangers of centralized government. The first volume of the book was published in 1835, the second in 1840. An ambitious work of great scope, generations have found something of interest in it. In America itself, the text is regarded as timeless. As the US historian Isaac Kramnick* has written: "For over a century and a half de Tocqueville's book has held up a mirror to Americans, allowing each generation to see themselves and their values in it."[1]

In *Democracy in America* Tocqueville describes and assesses American

> **❝** I confess that in America I saw more than America; I sought there the image of democracy itself, with its inclinations, its character, its prejudices, and its passions, in order to learn what we have to fear or hope from its progress. **❞**
>
> Alexis de Tocqueville, Democracy in America

politics in detail and makes uncannily accurate predictions about the fate of the United States.[2] The work also challenges conventional thinking about democracies. In the early nineteenth century most authors thought democracy would lead to anarchy,* a society where authority would not be recognized.[3] Tocqueville, though, was more concerned that democracy could lead to conformity. He focused on the potential consequences of a government that could have too much control over the lives of its citizens. Today Tocqueville's fears about too much government have been used to shape the debate about the role government should play in ensuring the welfare of its citizens.[4]

Author's Life
Alexis de Tocqueville (1805–1859) was born to a Catholic family of lower nobility in Normandy, France.[5] His parents lived through the French Revolution,* but were not themselves revolutionaries. They were, in fact, loyal followers of three French kings:

- Louis XVI,* who was executed in 1793 during the French Revolution.
- Louis XVIII* the brother of Louis XVI. He lived in exile during the Napoleonic era* at the start of the nineteenth century, but became king of France for a decade between 1814 and 1824.

- Charles X,* the younger brother of Louis XVI and XVIII. He came to the throne in 1824, but abdicated* in 1830 following a popular protest against his reign known as the July Revolution.

In 1823, seven years before the July Revolution, the 18-year-old Tocqueville went to Paris to study law.[6] Four years later, in 1827, his father arranged for him to be appointed as an apprentice judge at the Versailles court of law.[7] Here he became friends with his future traveling companion, Gustave de Beaumont,* a deputy public prosecutor.[8] The two men began to plan a visit to the United States. Tocqueville, then considering a career in politics and believing it was inevitable that France would become a democracy, was interested in visiting a country that had already made the transition to democratic government.

A democracy can be described as a system where a state's citizens have a say in that country's affairs, usually by voting to elect men and women to represent them in some kind of parliament. By the time of Tocqueville's visit, most white adult American men already had the right to vote in America. Tocqueville thought that if he could understand how the Americans had made this transition to democracy he would have insights that would help his political ambition. If nothing else, this knowledge would distinguish him from his peers.[9]

Tocqueville and Beaumont set sail for America in April 1831, arriving in New York the following month. For the best part of a year they explored America, visiting Michigan in the west, going south to New Orleans and traveling through Boston, New York and Philadelphia. Received as celebrities in the towns they visited, they met public officials such as professors, mayors, governors, and even the president at the time, Andrew Jackson.*[10] They also encountered many ordinary Americans, however, and did not miss an opportunity to question them and record the details of their conversations.[11]

Author's Background

The July Revolution of 1830 began in France nine months before Alexis de Tocqueville set sail for America. On July 25, 1830 the French king Charles X issued decrees that restricted press freedoms and excluded certain members of the middle class from the voting process.[12] Mobs soon gathered in Paris to denounce these decrees, and Charles fled to Britain.

With the end of the monarchy,* opinion was split over the form of government France should adopt. Students and workers wanted a democratic republic, with elected representatives and no king or queen. But the middle class argued for a constitutional monarchy,* with a head of state on the throne whose powers were limited in law.[13]

The middle class view won out. A new king—Louis-Philippe*— took the throne. Known as the citizen king ("roi-citoyen"), he made tentative moves towards developing a representative government.[14] The right to vote (suffrage*) was expanded and the middle class was allowed to vote as well as the aristocracy. French democracy was beginning to evolve.[15]

Although Tocqueville welcomed these developments, they troubled him, too. He feared that a consolidated and centralized government could lead to a new kind of despotism* in France, with a single entity ruling with absolute power.[16] Would a democratic state, by doing too much for its citizens, come to sap them of the character and resourcefulness that would allow them to think and act for themselves?

Tocqueville believed that the answer lay in somehow restraining central power. Local authorities such as the provincial parlements* (high courts) run by aristocrats had always been able to restrain central power.[17] But with the nobility all but destroyed, which bodies could limit centralized power now?[18]

These fears encouraged Tocqueville's interest in the United States, a democracy that had somehow avoided the danger of despotism. He wanted to understand how that country had achieved it, so that he could help France avoid any potential pitfalls on the road to democracy.[19]

NOTES

1 Alexis de Tocqueville, *Democracy in America*, trans. Gerald Bevan (London: Penguin, 2003), xii.

2 Tocqueville, *Democracy in America*, xxxvi.

3 Tocqueville, *Democracy in America*, xxv.

4 Steven Rathgeb Smith and Michael Lipsky, *Nonprofits for Hire: The Welfare State in the Age of Contracting* (Cambridge, MA: Harvard University Press, 2009), 26.

5 Tocqueville, *Democracy in America*, xii.

6 Tocqueville, *Democracy in America*, xiii.

7 Tocqueville, *Democracy in America*, xiii.

8 Tocqueville, *Democracy in America*, xiii.

9 Tocqueville, *Democracy in America*, xvii.

10 Tocqueville, *Democracy in America*, xix.

11 Tocqueville, *Democracy in America*, xix.

12 Tocqueville, *Democracy in America*, xv.

13 Tocqueville, *Democracy in America*, xv–xvi.

14 Tocqueville, *Democracy in America*, xvi.

15 Tocqueville, *Democracy in America*, xvi–xvii.

16 Tocqueville, *Democracy in America*, xviii.

17 Tocqueville, *Democracy in America*, xviii.

18 Tocqueville, *Democracy in America*, xviii.

19 Tocqueville, *Democracy in America*, xvii.

MODULE 2
ACADEMIC CONTEXT

KEY POINTS

- Comparative politics studies the influence of constitutions,* electoral systems and institutions on political outcomes. Political theory* considers how the political system actually works and how people can live good lives within it.

- When Alexis de Tocqueville was writing, comparative politics and political theory favored aristocratic* rather than democratic rule.

- Tocqueville was influenced by the philosophers Pascal,* Montesquieu,* and Rousseau.*

The Work In Its Context

Alexis de Tocqueville's *Democracy in America* can be seen as an exercise in the discipline of comparative politics. This term refers to the comparison of political patterns in two or more countries,[1] usually using only a small number of cases.[2] Comparative politics is concerned with the study of states and the similarities and differences of their forms of government.[3] It explores how constitutional organization, electoral systems, and institutional arrangements influence political and economic outcomes.[4] This understanding is reached by using *comparison*.[5] This comparative method is a means of discovering similarities among things that can vary. Comparative politics often deals with measurable issues, such as voter turnout, and how these vary in different countries and under different regimes.[6]

As well as using a comparative approach, Tocqueville's text also incorporates elements of political theory. He provides a theoretical

> **❝ A new science of politics is needed for a new world. ❞**
> Alexis de Tocqueville, *Democracy in America*

study of how the political system works and explores how human beings can "live good and just lives within a political community."[7] Political theory focuses on "the nature and structure of political practices, processes and institutions" and examines how the political world actually operates.[8] Political theory also has a philosophical element to it: those who practice political theory need to analyze the principles and beliefs that have helped to form particular political processes and structures.[9]

Overview of the Field

The Republic, written in about 380 B.C.E. by the Greek philosopher Plato,* is a major early work of comparative politics. In it, Plato compares five forms of government that evolve out of one another, in descending order of moral worth. These are as follows:

- **Aristocracy:*** Plato's preferred form of government, this is the government of the wise, motivated by reason and ruled by a philosopher king who strives for good.
- **Timocracy:*** described as a midpoint between aristocracy and oligarchy, timocracy is a government characterized by spirit and honor, where the ambitious timocratic man seeks power in order to satisfy his desire for public honor.
- **Oligarchy:*** a system of government rooted in wealth. In an oligarchy a rich minority rule over a poor majority.
- **Democracy:*** a system for the people founded on principles of liberty. In a democracy, governance is by all and equal.
- **Tyranny:*** a system driven by extreme appetites, where no one has any discipline and society exists in chaos.[10]

Plato argues against democracy in *The Republic*, reasoning that it was a form of government that would give people the freedom to do anything—including breaking the law. An aristocracy, on the other hand, would be ruled by a true statesman who would act according to what is right.[11]

Influenced by Plato, political theorists had also put forward the argument that democracies would "degenerate into anarchy* and disorder."[12] The German philosopher and political theorist Georg Wilhelm Friedrich Hegel,* for example, who died shortly before Tocqueville's text was published, was a vocal critic of democracy. Hegel argued that democracies were anarchic; that they disregarded the common good; that they failed to provide citizens with a meaningful voice; and that they were run by fools because citizens lack the expertise to govern.[13]

Further, Hegel contended that democracies would make freedom insecure because new regimes could overturn existing rules and orders. When every citizen claimed to have a right to contribute to new laws, legal systems would fall into disarray. As he put it: "No one would be able to claim the protection of the laws."[14]

Hegel also believed it would become difficult to pursue practical, workable policies in a democracy because the citizens of the state would not know what they really wanted.[15] Rather than supporting democracy, Hegel preferred the system of a hereditary monarch* who would propose laws—with the consent of his cabinet* of advisors—to an elected assembly.[16]

Academic Influences

In a letter to a friend, Tocqueville wrote: "There are three men with whom I spend a little time each day, Pascal, Montesquieu and Rousseau."[17]

Tocqueville borrowed the idea that people could be capable of both brutality and greatness from the first of these three men: the seventeenth-century French philosopher Blaise Pascal.[18] Pascal came to the conclusion that political life would be dominated by "madmen," because only madmen would want this kind of power. Tocqueville, however, interpreted Pascal's ideas as meaning that rulers *may* be capable of moderation and justice.[19]

The second of the three, Montesquieu, was an eighteenth-century French philosopher who studied different political structures. Tocqueville adopted his methods of political inquiry, investigating societies rather than types of government.[20] He agreed with Montesquieu that the powers invested in the state should be divided between different groups rather than being concentrated in one particular person or group. The state powers he was referring to were the powers to make and implement rules and to judge whether those rules had been followed. Giving different groups the responsibility for these functions would help to create an internal system of checks and balances that would moderate state power. This would in turn allow liberty to flourish.[21]

The third man Tocqueville "spent time with" every day was the eighteenth-century Genevan philosopher Jean-Jacques Rousseau, who seems to have influenced Tocqueville's ideas about freedom. Rousseau was interested in how a political community could be established within a commercial society. He argued that, for this to work, individuals would have to agree to laws that would actually curb some of their own activities. But they would only do this if the laws benefited them overall. Like Rousseau, Tocqueville saw freedom in terms of "active participation in the general will."[22] As he said: "Freedom consists of obedience to self-made law."[23] In short, it wasn't down to the government simply to impose those laws. The people had to actively want them.

All three of the philosophers referred to by Tocqueville were interested in what "liberty" and "justice" actually mean. They discussed the question of *who* should rule. *Democracy in America* did the same thing.

NOTES

1   Kenneth Newton and Jan W. van Deth, *Foundations of Comparative Politics* (Cambridge: Cambridge University Press, 2009), 4.

2   Newton and van Deth, *Comparative Politics*, 13.

3   Newton and van Deth, *Comparative Politics*, 13.

4   Gretchen Helmke and Steven Levitsky, "Informal Institutions and Comparative Politics," *Perspectives on Politics* 2, no. 4 (2004): 725.

5   Arend Lijphart, "Comparative Politics and the Comparative Method," *The American Political Science Review* 65, no. 3 (1971): 682.

6   Newton and Van Deth, *Comparative Politics*, 7.

7   Richard J Bernstein, *The Restructuring of Social and Political Theory* (Philadelphia: University of Pennsylvania Press, 1978), xxii.

8   David Held, *Political Theory and the Modern State* (London: Wiley, 2013), 3.

9   Held, *Political Theory*, 3.

10 See book VIII of Plato, *The Republic*, ed. G. R. F. Ferrari, trans. Tom Griffith (Cambridge: Cambridge University Press, 2000)

11 Ernest Barker, *The Political Thought of Plato and Aristotle* (Chelmsford: Courier Corporation, 2012), 167.

12 Alexis de Tocqueville, *Democracy in America,* trans. Gerald Bevan (London: Penguin, 2003), xxv.

13 Thom Brooks, "Plato, Hegel, and Democracy," *Bulletin of the Hegel Society of Great Britain* 53, no. 54 (2006): 8.

14 Michael P. Allen, "Hegel between Non-Domination and Expressive Freedom Capabilities, Perspectives, Democracy," *Philosophy and Social Criticism* 32, no. 4 (2006): 498.

15 Allen, "Hegel," 499.

16 Brooks, "Plato, Hegel, and Democracy," 6.

17 David W. Carrithers, "Montesquieu and Tocqueville as Philosophical Historians," in *Montlsquleu and His Legacy*, ed. Rebecca Kingston (New York: State University Press of New York, Albany 2009), 149.

18 Peter Augustine Lawler, *The Restless Mind: Alexis de Tocqueville on the Origin and Perpetuation of Human Liberty* (Lanham: Rowman & Littlefield, 1993), 81.

19 Lawler, *Restless Mind,* 82–83.

20 Lawler, *Restless Mind,* 150.

21 Lawler, *Restless Mind*.

22 John C. Koritansky, "Decentralization and Civic Virtue in Tocqueville's 'New Science of Politics'," *Publius* 5, no. 3 (1975): 66.

23 Koritansky, "Decentralization," 66.

MODULE 3
THE PROBLEM

KEY POINTS

- Tocqueville's contemporaries were concerned with how best to implement representative government.*

- Other thinkers of the time rejected democracy* as a way to introduce representative government in France. Some believed the English parliamentary system should be used as a model.

- Tocqueville thought that democracy might be beneficial and used the United States rather than England as the subject of his study.

Core Question

"What are the lessons that the French might learn from the American experiment with democracy?" asks Alexis de Tocqueville in *Democracy in America*.[1] With this question in mind, he discusses the benefits and potential dangers of democracy itself.

His interest in the United States stemmed from his belief that it was a country that had successfully introduced democracy—a positive contrast to the experience of his own country, France, where a democratic revolution had been proven to be unsuccessful. According to Tocqueville, French democracy had been "abandoned to its primitive instincts"[2] while in America it had "been able to grow freely and develop its legislation peacefully by moving in harmony with the country's customs."[3]

In the period Tocqueville researched and wrote the work, it seemed probable that democracy would take root in France. He described democratization as an "irresistible revolution" that

> ❝ Democracy has thus been abandoned to its primitive instincts; it has grown like those children who, deprived of a father's care, are left to fend for themselves in the streets of our towns and who come to learn only the vices and wretchedness of our society. ❞
>
> Alexis de Tocqueville, *Democracy in America*.

represented the will of God,[4] even if France had, so far, only experienced "democracy minus everything to lessen its defects or to promote its natural advantages."[5] To remedy this, Tocqueville wanted his country to learn the lessons of America's democratic success.

The Participants

Even before Tocqueville went to the United States in April 1831, a debate had already begun in France about representative government. On one side were the Ultras,* a group of hard-line supporters of royal power who wanted to strengthen the position of the monarchy.*[6] On the other were the Doctrinaires,* a group drawn from France's political and intellectual elite. Although the Doctrinaires wanted a system of representative government,[7] they were not all in favor of democracy. Instead they wanted a form of government where the interests of society as a whole would be represented and protected.[8] As a part of this general view, they argued that the Charter of 1814*—a legal text drawn up when the country's Bourbon monarchy was restored and which limited the monarch's power—should be properly applied.[9] The Doctrinaires also wanted two parliamentary chambers with members elected by a limited group of people, primarily from educated backgrounds and with property.[10]

Occupying the middle ground between the Ultras and the Doctrinaires was the French writer and politician François-René de Chateaubriand.* He initially supported the restoration of the monarchy, arguing that it offered France the possibility of peace and prosperity in an era which he thought to be dominated by impotence and a crisis of authority. On another level, Chateaubriand depended on the support of monarchical pensions. However, he believed that the monarch should reign, but not govern. Ministers would govern and would be "responsible before parliament and dependent on the support of majority opinion."[1]

The Contemporary Debate

Despite backing representative government, leading members of the Doctrinaires were not in favor of democracy. The leader of the group, the statesman Pierre-Paul Royer-Collard* argued that society should not be seen in terms of individuals, "the numerical assemblage of individuals and wills," but as groups of "legitimate interests."[12] He wanted to retain the aristocracy (and with it a degree of social inequality) because without it, French democracy would rest on the dominance of the people. Royer-Collard thought this would lead to anarchy,* tyranny* and despotism.*[13]

Another Doctrinaire, the historian François Guizot,* argued for a meritocracy: a system where people progress according to their talents rather than their class or their wealth. He said there should be civil and legal equality in society and this would enable individuals to make the most of their talents.[14] This social mobility would ensure that power passed into the hands of those with superior talents.[15] Guizot did not support representative government based on the will of the majority.[16] He believed that there should be elections but that only independently minded and intellectually developed men should be allowed to vote in them.[17] His preferred model was the electoral system of fourteenth-century England, which he identified as following principles of freedom, direct election, and open voting.[18] Nevertheless, Guizot accepted that democracy was very appealing to the French. Recognizing that it could not be held back, he said that democracy should be "contained and controlled."[19]

NOTES

1   Alexis de Tocqueville, *Democracy in America,* trans. Gerald Bevan (London: Penguin, 2003), 23.

2   Tocqueville, *Democracy in America*, 16.

3   Tocqueville, *Democracy in America*, 23.

4   Tocqueville, *Democracy in America*, 15.

5   Tocqueville, *Democracy in America*, 17.

6   Jeremy Jennings, "Revolution and the Republic," *A History of Political Thought in France since the Eighteenth Century* (Oxford: Oxford University Press, 2011), 168; Aurelian Craiutu, "Between Scylla and Charybdis: The 'Strange' Liberalism of the French Doctrinaires," *History of European Ideas* 24, nos. 4–5 (1998): 243.

7   Jennings, "Revolution and the Republic," 169.

8   Craiutu, "Scylla and Charybdis," 256.

9   Jennings, "Revolution and the Republic," 167–68.

10 Jennings, "Revolution and the Republic," 167–68

11 Jennings, "Revolution and the Republic," 169.

12 Jennings, "Revolution and the Republic," 172.

13 Jennings, "Revolution and the Republic," 172/

14 Jennings, "Revolution and the Republic,"174.

15 Jennings, "Revolution and the Republic," 175.

16 Jennings, "Revolution and the Republic," 175.

17 Jennings, "Revolution and the Republic,"175–76.

18 Jennings, "Revolution and the Republic," 177.

19 Jennings, "Revolution and the Republic," 180.

MODULE 4
THE AUTHOR'S CONTRIBUTION

KEY POINTS

- Alexis de Tocqueville believed that democracy in France was inevitable. He wanted to learn lessons from the American experience that could be applied to France.

- Tocqueville's view departed from the views of previous thinkers who had argued against democracy, or used England as the subject of their studies.

- Tocqueville expanded on the ideas of his contemporaries, who argued that democracy needed to be controlled. He also warned against an overly centralized government.

Author's Aims

In *Democracy in America,* Alexis de Tocqueville explored ideas of representative government.* But his inquiry was original because it focused on democracy.

Although the Doctrinaires,* a French political group that counted the statesmen Pierre-Paul Royer-Collard* and François Guizot* among its members, agreed that the rule of a monarchy should give way to a form of representative government, they nevertheless opposed democracy. Their argument was that it would lead to tyranny* and despotism.*[1] In this they differed from Tocqueville, who reasoned that democracy might promote a respect for the law and a mutual respect between citizens.[2] The Doctrinaires focused on the principle of representation and were concerned with exactly who in society would be fit to participate in elections. Tocqueville's view was that representative institutions had to be democratic if they were representative of the people.[3]

Tocqueville's inquiry was also quite original in its focus on the

66 The democracy prevailing over American societies appeared to me to be advancing rapidly to power in Europe. That was the moment I conceived the idea for the book that lies before the reader. 99

Alexis de Tocqueville, *Democracy in America*

United States as a model of government. Royer-Collard did not look for solutions outside France, while Guizot thought that the French government should model itself on the electoral and parliamentary systems of medieval England.[4] Tocqueville rejected Guizot's ideas on the grounds that the English aristocracy was already losing influence to democracy.[5]

Approach

In his introduction to *Democracy in America*, Tocqueville reflects on the equality of social conditions in the United States. Suggesting that similar trends towards equality were emerging in Europe, he writes that "the democracy prevailing over American societies appeared to be advancing rapidly to power in Europe." Indeed, he writes that realizing this was "the moment I conceived the idea for the book."[6]

Tocqueville argues that France's democratic revolution had not been successful. Believing that democracy *had* been established successfully in America, he wrote: "It is not simply, therefore, to satisfy a curiosity … that I have examined America; my aim has been to discover lessons from which we may profit."[7] In the first volume of *Democracy in America,* Tocqueville describes and assesses the legislative and executive powers in the United States. He also discusses the advantages and disadvantages of America's laws and public affairs. In the second volume Tocqueville explores the influence that equal social conditions have on civil society, habits, ideas, and manners.[8]

His text represented the first study of its kind on the United States.

In 1838 the American magazine *Knickerbocker** reviewed *Democracy in America*. It praised Tocqueville's work, saying Americans had "been an enigma to the world; our author has at last partly solved it."[9]

Contribution In Context

It is difficult to assess the impact of other political theorists on *Democracy in America* because Alexis de Tocqueville did not usually acknowledge his influences.[10] Nonetheless, it is likely that some of Tocqueville's ideas were shaped by two of the Doctrinaires, François Guizot and Pierre-Paul Royer-Collard. Both Guizot and Royer-Collard argued that the social conditions in France were changing and that political institutions had to adapt to that change.[11] Tocqueville uses a similar line of reasoning in *Democracy in America*.[12]

Guizot was both a historian and a statesman and Tocqueville is known to have attended his lectures between 1828 and 1830.[13] Guizot argued that since democracy could not simply be suppressed, it must be contained and controlled.[14] Tocqueville, who agreed that democracy was inevitable, argued that the "first of the duties that are at this time imposed upon those who direct our affairs is to educate democracy."[15] If the people were to hold power, he argued, they needed to understand the responsibilities that came with it.

Tocqueville also corresponded with Royer-Collard,[16] who argued that local liberties should be preserved. Royer-Collard warned that "centralization will be the natural government."[17] But the importance of keeping a balance between the local and the central is a theme that Tocqueville expands on in *Democracy in America*.

Guizot and Royer-Collard took the view that democracy could potentially lead to tyranny and despotism.[18] In *Democracy in America*, Tocqueville discusses two concepts that may have had their roots in these ideas. The first is what Tocqueville called "the tyranny of the majority:"* the possibility that minority voices may find no room for expression in a democracy. Tocqueville's second concept is "the democratic despot:"* a centralized state, that, although well meaning, controls its citizens to such a degree that they lose their capacity to think and act for themselves.

NOTES

1 Jeremy Jennings, "Revolution and the Republic," *A History of Political Thought in France since the Eighteenth Century* (Oxford: Oxford University Press, 2011), 80, 172.

2 Alexis de Tocqueville, *Democracy in America*, vol. 1, trans. Henry Reeve (Washington: Regnery Publishing, 2003), 17.

3 Tocqueville, *Democracy in America,* trans. Reeve, xxvi.

4 Jeremy Jennings, "Revolution and the Republic," *A History of Political Thought in France since the Eighteenth Century* (Oxford: Oxford University Press, 2011), 175.

5 Jennings, "Revolution and the Republic," 182–83.

6 Alexis de Tocqueville, *Democracy in America,* trans. Gerald Bevan (London: Penguin, 2003), 11.

7 Tocqueville, *Democracy in America*, trans. Bevan, 23.

8 Tocqueville, *Democracy in America*, trans. Bevan, 24.

9 Tocqueville, *Democracy in America*, trans. Bevan, xiii.

10 James T. Schleifer, *The Chicago Companion to de Tocqueville's Democracy in America* (Chicago: University of Chicago Press, 2012), 37.

11 Aurelian Craiutu, "Between Scylla and Charybdis: The 'Strange' Liberalism of the French Doctrinaires," *History of European Ideas* 24, nos. 4–5 (1998): 250.

12 Craiutu, "Scylla and Charybdis, 250..

13 Jennings, "Revolution and the Republic," 181.

14 Jennings, "Revolution and the Republic," 181.

15 Tocqueville, *Democracy in America*, trans. Bevan, 16.

16 Tocqueville, *Democracy in America*, trans. Reeve, xxxiii.

17 Aurelian Craiutu, "Tocqueville and the Political Thought of the French Doctrinaires (Guizot, Royer-Collard, Rémusat)," *History of Political Thought* 20, no. 3 (1999): 480.

18 Jennings, "Revolution and the Republic," 172, 80.

SECTION 2
IDEAS

MODULE 5
MAIN IDEAS

KEY POINTS

- Alexis de Tocqueville wanted to outline the benefits and pitfalls of democracy.*

- He wanted to learn from the American experience to help France move towards democracy.

- He wanted to avoid the tyranny* and despotism* he felt might come with democracy and centralized power.

Key Themes

In *Democracy in America,* Alexis de Tocqueville explores the key theme of how the successful lessons of American democracy might be applied to France. His work "offers a political program for sustaining democratic societies that are prosperous, stable and free."[1] He believes that "a new political science is needed for a totally new world."[2] He sees his central task as isolating the advantages and disadvantages of democracy and then explaining how to enhance the advantages and avoid the disadvantages.[3]

Tocqueville recognizes that democracy has the potential to pose unique threats to liberty, warning that the "tyranny of the majority"* has the potential to be dangerous.[4] As he points out: "It is the very essence of democratic government that the power of the majority should be absolute."[5] But this gives the majority "immense actual power and a power of opinion almost as great."[6] Since elected representatives are appointed directly by the people and only hold office for a limited term, these representatives are in many ways forced to bow to public opinion.[7]

Tocqueville argues that the majority—taken as a collective

> ❝ When, therefore, I see the right and capacity to enact everything given to any authority whatsoever, whether it be called people or king, democracy or aristocracy, whether exercised in a monarchy or a republic, I say: the seed of tyranny lies there and I seek to live under different laws. ❞
>
> Alexis de Tocqueville, *Democracy in America*

whole—is as open to corruption as any individual. If "an all-powerful man can abuse his power" then the same must hold true of the majority.[8] Likewise, he warns of the dangers of an omnipresent state, arguing that "an extreme form of centralization of political power ultimately weakens society and enfeebles government."[9]

Exploring The Ideas

In *Democracy in America*, Tocqueville identifies the problems that a democracy might present and offers ideas about how we might guard against them.

To restrain the tyranny of the majority, he calls for powers to be separated. He says that legislature (the body of elected people who are empowered to make laws) should be distinct from the executive authority (the branch with the power to enforce the law), and that the judiciary (the system of courts) should be independent.[10] Tocqueville did not claim that America had experienced tyranny, but he was concerned that, even there, there were not enough safeguards against it.[11]

Tocqueville does, however, highlight two factors that he feels curb the tyranny of the majority in the United States. The first is America's lack of centralized administration. When the federal government of the United States issued a command, for example, it had to rely on local municipal bodies to ensure that it was executed. This system prevented the main government from directly regulating all aspects of its citizens' lives.[12]

Secondly, Tocqueville views the legal profession as a kind of guardian, protecting society against tyranny. Tocqueville sees lawyers and judges as lovers of order, rules, and stability, armed with the right to declare laws unconstitutional.[13] He believes lawyers and judges play a crucial role in helping to moderate the excesses of democracy.[14]

Tocqueville considers ways of guarding against excessive governmental centralization in Volume One of *Democracy in America*. He returns to the idea in the second volume, outlining his beliefs about the consequences of excessive government centralization. Tocqueville imagines the rise of democratic despotism in the new world, describing a protective power that takes care of its citizens' needs to such an extent that "it reduces each nation to nothing more than a flock of timid and hardworking animals with the government as shepherd."[15] The despotic democracy "is absolute, meticulous, ordered, provident, and kindly disposed."[16] Because this kind of despotism removes "the bother of thinking and the troubles of life," its citizens will ultimately end up peacefully enslaved.[17] This idea is original; previously it had been thought that democracy would lead to anarchy.*[18]

Language And Expression

It was Alexis de Tocqueville's desire for a political career that drove his decision to travel to the United States in 1831. He believed that knowledge of American affairs would be to his advantage on his return to France[19] and, judging from the sophisticated language he used in writing the book, it seems that he intended its audience to be France's influential intellectual elite.

He began to write *Democracy in America* on his return to France in February 1832. After the first volume was published in 1835, Tocqueville was invited to join the Académie Française*—the official body that discusses all matters regarding the French language. This was the highest honor France could grant to an artist or intellectual.[20] The Académie Française has only 40 members at a time, known as *immortels* ("immortals"). Tocqueville was only 36 when he was invited to join them, which may further suggest that Tocqueville's text was intended for—and was appreciated by—a highly educated audience.

The modern reader may feel that some of Tocqueville's language is offensive; his choice of words belongs to a very different era. Native Americans are referred to as "savages" and African-Americans as "Negroes" (words used and accepted without any comment at all in the nineteenth century).[21] Yet despite the language he used, Tocqueville's ideas were progressive. He argued that slavery was degrading and that Native Americans had been exploited at the hands of the white settlers, observations in line with modern thinking. The modern reader may perhaps have to make allowances for terminology that is usually considered unacceptable today.

NOTES

1 Tocqueville, *Democracy in America*, trans. Gerald Bevan (London: Penguin, 2003), 16

2 Tocqueville, *Democracy in America*, 16.

3 James T. Schleifer, *The Chicago Companion to de Tocqueville's Democracy in America* (Chicago: University of Chicago Press, 2012), 50.

4 Schleifer, *Chicago Companion*, 50.

5 Tocqueville, *Democracy in America*, 287.

6 Tocqueville, *Democracy in America*, 290.

7 Tocqueville, *Democracy in America*, 288.

8 Tocqueville, *Democracy in America*, 293.

9 Tocqueville, *Democracy in America*, 787.

10 Tocqueville, *Democracy in America*, 295–96.

11 Tocqueville, *Democracy in America*, 296.

12 Tocqueville, *Democracy in America*, 306.

13 Tocqueville, *Democracy in America*, 313–14.

14 Tocqueville, *Democracy in America*, 307.

15 Tocqueville, *Democracy in America*, 805–6.

16 Tocqueville, *Democracy in America*, 805.

17 Tocqueville, *Democracy in America*, 806.

18 Tocqueville, *Democracy in America*, xxv.

19 Tocqueville, *Democracy in America*, xvii.

20 Tocqueville, *Democracy in America*, xxxvii.

21 Tocqueville, *Democracy in America*, xxxv.

MODULE 6
SECONDARY IDEAS

KEY POINTS

- Alexis de Tocqueville argues that a strong civil society* is good for democracy.*
- Tocqueville also argues that civil society may reduce the power of the government and even halt abuses of state power.
- Tocqueville has even been cited in a modern context when scholars have been investigating links between equality and democracy.

Other Ideas

Alexis de Tocqueville's observations on America's civil society (a community of citizens joined together by common interests and common activities) remain an important part of *Democracy in America*. He devotes a chapter to the importance of civic associations in the United States, noting: "Americans of all ages, conditions, and all dispositions constantly unite together."[1] In addition to commercial and industrial associations, American citizens also belong to associations that are "religious, moral, serious, futile, very general and very specialized, large and small."[2] These associations bind together to achieve all sorts of aims: from holding festivals and celebrations to distributing books to constructing hospitals and prisons.[3]

For Tocqueville, this associational involvement is clearly linked to a strong democracy. He says: "The most democratic country in the world is that in which men have in our time perfected the art of pursuing in concert the aim of their common desires and have applied this new technique to the greatest number of objectives."[4] Tocqueville

> ❝ In short, giving, volunteering, and joining are mutually reinforcing and habit-forming—as de Tocqueville put it, 'the habits of the heart. ❞
>
> Robert Putnam, *Bowling Alone*

believed it was important that associations should be formed by citizens rather than by the government. He argues that this is essential for the country's moral and intellectual well-being.[5] By choosing to participate with others in order to achieve common goals, individual Americans showed they had initiative. They proved that the state had not succumbed to democratic despotism,* removing "the bother of thinking" from its citizens.[6]

Exploring The Ideas

Tocqueville's idea that civic associations could act as a safeguard against the excessive accumulation of power by a centralized democratic state was original, and developed as a result of his travels in the United States. He believed that the high level of civic engagement displayed in America was unlike anything seen in Europe, where new initiatives would be spearheaded by the government or by a noble lord rather than by "common" citizens.[7]

Although his discussion of associations is relatively short—just one chapter in Volume Two—it is important for the idea that an association, "in defending its particular rights against the exigencies of power, saves common freedoms" by empowering its members. Tocqueville argues that, "A political, industrial, commercial, or even scientific and literary association equals an educated and powerful citizen who cannot be persuaded at will nor suppressed in some shadowy corner and who saves the liberties of all by defending its own rights against the demands of the government."[8]

Overlooked

One frequently overlooked aspect of Alexis de Tocqueville's text is his discussion of the importance of equality in a successful democracy.

The opening line of *Democracy in America* is: "Of all of the novel things which attracted my attention during my stay in the United States, none struck me more forcibly than the equality of social conditions."[9] He goes on to discuss equality throughout the text, arguing both that it leads to a preference for democracy and that it had a role in leading America to independence from Britain. In a hierarchical system, some men are wholly dependent on others within the community. In a democracy, on the other hand, individuals operate independently. Tocqueville argues that a man living with equality will choose a form of government where he can elect the leader and control that leader's actions.[10]

It is possible that Tocqueville's observations on the equality of social conditions may have struck readers as unimportant in the past, when the living conditions of Americans were more equal. But income inequality in the United States today is at its highest levels since the Great Depression of 1929,* a fact that has led some economists to speculate that income inequality harms economic growth. The economist Annie Lowrey's article "Income Inequality May Take Toll on Growth" in the *New York Times* of October 16, 2012 is a good example.

One thinker who has attempted to refocus attention on equality is Terry Lynn Karl,* a professor of politics at Stanford University. Citing Tocqueville, Karl argues that income inequality in Latin America—which is seen as the most unequal region in the world—may have a negative impact on its emerging democracies.[11] But Karl's attempt to refocus attention on this area of Tocqueville's text has not been successful. While other authors have focused on the role inequality plays in democratic instability, they have not cited Tocqueville in their arguments.[12]

NOTES

1 Alexis de Tocqueville, *Democracy in America* (London: Penguin, 2003), 596.

2 Tocqueville, *Democracy in America*, 596.

3 Tocqueville, *Democracy in America*, 596.

4 Tocqueville, *Democracy in America*, 596.

5 Tocqueville, *Democracy in America*, 598.

6 Tocqueville, *Democracy in America*, 806.

7 Tocqueville, *Democracy in America*, 596.

8 Tocqueville, *Democracy in America*, 811.

9 Tocqueville, *Democracy in America*, 11.

10 Tocqueville, *Democracy in America*, 775–76.

11 Terry Lynn Karl, "Economic Inequality and Democratic Instability," *Journal of Democracy* 11, no. 1 (2000): 149–50.

12 See, for example, Robert R. Kaufman, "The Political Effects of Inequality in Latin America: Some Inconvenient Facts," *Comparative Politics* 41, no. 3 (2009); David Altman and Rossana Castiglioni, "Democratic Quality and Human Development in Latin America: 1972–2001," *Canadian Journal of Political Science* 42, no. 2 (2009).

MODULE 7
ACHIEVEMENT

KEY POINTS

- Alexis de Tocqueville set out to learn lessons about American democracy that would benefit France. In doing so, he established a political program for a prosperous, stable, and free democracy.

- His careful analysis of the upsides and the downsides of democracy helped him achieve his goals.

- Although *Democracy in America* was written for a French audience, its influence has been most lasting in the United States.

Assessing The Argument

In the introduction to *Democracy in America*, Alexis de Tocqueville writes: "It is not simply, therefore, to satisfy a curiosity … that I have examined America; my aim has been to discover lessons from which we may profit."[1]

The first part of his book, he goes on to explain, discusses the advantages and disadvantages of America's laws and public affairs. The second part aims to explore the influence of equal social conditions on civil society,* habits, ideas, and manners.[2]

Although Tocqueville clearly outlines his aims to the reader, the extent to which these aims are realized varies. He is perhaps most successful in his aim of drawing lessons from America's successful experience of democracy when he explicitly contrasts Europe with America. His discussion of administrative centralization, for example, must have been of particular interest to his European readers.[3]

At other times, however, Tocqueville discusses aspects of American

> **❝** For over a century and a half de Tocqueville's book has held up a mirror to Americans, allowing each generation to see themselves and their values in it **❞**
> Isaac Kramnick,* introduction to *Democracy in America*

life as phenomena that stand alone. The lessons of his discussion of slavery, for example,[4] are harder to apply to a European setting. Similarly, Tocqueville warns his readers that democracy may lead to the rise of democratic despotism:* a state so powerful that it infantilizes its citizens. But he does not offer any solutions as to how to guard against this risk; he offers a warning rather than a lesson.

Achievement In Context

The first volume of *Democracy in America* owes its positive reception, in part, to the political changes taking place in France when the book was published. There were concerns about the stability of King Louis-Philippe's* regime in 1835; Tocqueville's claim that democracy was inevitable highlighted these concerns.[5]

Clearly, the book was topical. Shortly after it was published there were calls for more equality in France.[6] Its focus on the United States was of interest to French republicans who were debating whether the American model should be used in a French republic.[7]

The success of the second volume, published in 1840, was hampered by both commercial decisions and changed political circumstances. Tocqueville initially printed the work in an expensive format, affordable only to the elite,[8] which meant that it sold more slowly than the first volume. And King Louis-Philippe's regime was more secure than it had been five years earlier. Public opinion, in other words, was no longer focused on the idea of democracy.[9] By 1848, however, there was a surge in interest in Volume Two as Louis-Philippe was overthrown and France's Second Republic* was established with

Louis-Napoleon Bonaparte as president.*[10] A new publisher offered *Democracy in America* in a cheaper format, too, making it more readily available.[11]

Limitations

As the title suggests, *Democracy in America* focuses on the United States and most of Tocqueville's observations are based on the nine months he spent there. Besides describing and assessing American politics in detail, Tocqueville speculates on the future of the nation. He makes predictions about the fate of the union; slavery; the Supreme Court;* and the size of the population. Many of his predictions have proved to be uncannily accurate. It is perhaps because of this that *Democracy in America* has been so influential in the United States.[12] In America, Tocqueville's text is regarded as timeless, appealing to Americans from different generations and from both ends of the political spectrum.

It could be argued, however, that *Democracy in America* lacks universal appeal. Although some of Tocqueville's arguments would be relevant to any democracy—for instance his thoughts about the potential dangers of a despotic centralized power—others are entirely specific to the United States. These include his argument that that the appeal of religion in America is based on the country's separation of Church and state.[13] From the 1780s onwards, religious freedom had come to prevail in America as a result of the separation between the rights of religion and civil authority. By the 1830s, foreign observers generally regarded the separation of church and state as the unanimously accepted American approach.

This American bias may explain why the book has been less influential in France, with some critics seeing Tocqueville as "too American" and an "apologist for a foreign model."[14]

NOTES

1   Alexis de Tocqueville, *Democracy in America* (London: Penguin, 2003), 23.

2   Tocqueville, *Democracy in America*, 24.

3   Tocqueville, *Democracy in America*, 104–5.

4   Tocqueville, *Democracy in America*, 440–41.

5   Françoise Mélonio, *Tocqueville and the French* (Charlottesville: University of Virginia Press, 1998), 35.

6   Mélonio, *Tocqueville*, 35.

7   Mélonio, *Tocqueville,* 34.

8   Mélonio, *Tocqueville*, 66–67.

9   Mélonio, *Tocqueville,* 67.

10   Mélonio, *Tocqueville,* 67.

11   Mélonio, *Tocqueville,* 67.

12   Tocqueville, Democracy in America, xxxvi.

13   Tocqueville, Democracy in America, xxxiv.

14   Françoise Mélonio, "Tocqueville and the French," in *The Cambridge Companion to de Tocqueville*, ed. Cheryl B. Welch (New York: Cambridge University Press, 2006), 55, 337.

MODULE 8
PLACE IN THE AUTHOR'S WORK

KEY POINTS

- Alexis de Tocqueville was concerned with the danger posed by the excessive centralization of power both in his writing and in his political life.

- Both *Democracy in America* and Tocqueville's later work, *The Ancien Régime and the Revolution,* focus on how a country makes the transition to democracy.

- *Democracy in America* is Tocqueville's best known and most widely read book.

Positioning

In *Democracy in America,* Alexis de Tocqueville explores his fear of a despotic,* centralized power. He returns to the idea in *The Ancien Régime and the Revolution,* his second great work, published 16 years after *Democracy in America* in 1856.

In *The Ancien Régime,* Tocqueville traces the history of French politics, showing how power had become increasingly centralized and blaming the Enlightenment* philosophers Voltaire* and Rousseau* for helping to legitimize the process.[1] Rousseau had argued that power should be in the hands of the people. Voltaire had argued that power should be in the hands of an enlightened monarch. Yet, crucially, both had supported the idea of *concentrated* power.

Tocqueville's fear about centralization was not just expressed in his books, however. After the abdication of the French king Louis-Philippe* following the revolution of 1848,* Tocqueville was elected to a committee tasked with drafting a new French constitution.*[2] He proposed a system of checks and balances that would help to prevent

" Tocqueville saw himself as the thinker of the democratic transition, and unless we keep that objective in mind, we cannot understand what ties his various works together. **"**

Françoise Mélonio, "Tocqueville and the French," in *The Cambridge Companion to de Tocqueville*

the centralized state from assuming absolute power.[3]

Another of Tocqueville's recurring themes was slavery. He had already condemned slavery in *Democracy in America* in 1835. But in 1839 he was elected to the lower chamber of the French Parliament, the Chamber of Deputies,* and here he made speeches publicly labeling slavery a moral abomination. He called for it to be abolished in the French colonies*[4] and wrote six articles for the French daily newspaper *Le Siècle* explaining why slavery should be outlawed.[5] He served on a parliamentary commission investigating the practice and even argued that the Chamber of Deputies should set a date for the emancipation of slaves.[6]

Integration

At first glance, Alexis de Tocqueville's two works—*Democracy in America* and *The Ancien Régime and the Revolution*—may appear to have little in common. *Democracy in America* has a contemporary focus while *The Ancien Régime and the Revolution* is a historical study, examining French society before the revolution and focusing on the causes of that revolution.

The two works have similarities, however. Both are concerned with the transition of a state from a monarchy* to a democracy.*[7] *Democracy in America* asks how lessons from the American experiment with democracy can be applied to France. *The Ancien Régime and the Revolution* considers the ways in which absolute monarchies in Europe complicated the establishment of democracies.[8] Both texts reveal a concern about despotism.* Whereas *Democracy in America* outlines the possible rise of democratic despotism,* *The Ancien Régime and the Revolution* discusses why successive French revolutions ended in despotism.*[9]

Arguably, the intention behind both books was to support the rise of a healthy democracy. In *The Ancien Régime and the Revolution* Tocqueville asks similar questions to the ones in *Democracy in America*. How can liberty be reconciled with equality? Why was democracy in America peaceful, while France was plagued with revolutions?[10] The entire body of Tocqueville's work can be seen as a reflection on how to manage the transition to democracy.[11]

Significance

Democracy in America was Tocqueville's first major literary achievement.[12] Despite his relative youth and his lack of celebrity, the book was an extraordinary success. It was hailed as a masterpiece,[13] was praised by American and French reviewers alike, and led to Tocqueville being invited to join the Académie Française,* the elite group chosen to safeguard the French language, at the age of 36.

But despite the initial enthusiasm the work generated in his homeland, French interest in Tocqueville had begun to wane by the 1900s.[14] And as the United States began to industrialize and take in immigrants, Tocqueville's portrait of the country seemed less relevant.[15] There was a revival of interest in *Democracy in America* in the mid-twentieth century, however, as political theorists* began to reference the book. The well-known American political theorist Robert Dahl used ideas from Tocqueville as he developed his theory of democratic pluralism, a political system where there is more than one center of power.[16]

Throughout *Democracy in America*, Tocqueville makes predictions about the future of America. Some of these predictions—Tocqueville's view that the United States and Russia would turn into rival superpowers,* for example—ended up being right.[17] Some have been disproved, however. Tocqueville claims, for example, that if "freedom is refused the Negroes of the South, they will end up by seizing it themselves." This, of course, didn't happen; it was a civil war between states of the American north and south that eventually led to the abolition of slavery.[18]

Democracy in America remains Tocqueville's most famous work. His second text, *The Ancien Régime and the Revolution*, has attracted comparatively little interest.[19]

NOTES

1   Alexis de Tocqueville, *Democracy in America* (London: Penguin, 2003), xi.

2   Tocqueville, *Democracy in America*, xxxix.

3   Tocqueville, *Democracy in America*, xxxix.

4   Tocqueville, *Democracy in America*, xxxvii–xxxviii.

5   Sally Gershman, "Alexis de Tocqueville and Slavery," *French Historical Studies* 9, no. 3 (1976): 479.

6   Alexis de Tocqueville, *Writings on Empire and Slavery*, trans. Jennifer Pitts (Baltimore: JHU Press, 2001), xxix.

7   Françoise Mélonio, *Tocqueville and the French* (Charlottesville: University of Virginia Press, 1998), 338.

8   Mélonio, *Tocqueville*, 338.

9   Mélonio, *Tocqueville*, 344.

10 Mélonio, *Tocqueville* and the French, 334.

11 Mélonio, *Tocqueville*, 345.

12 Tocqueville, *Democracy in America*, xxi–xxii.

13 Tocqueville, *Democracy in America*, xxiii.

14 Cheryl B. Welch, "Tocqueville in the Twenty-First Century," in *The Cambridge Companion to de Tocqueville*, ed. Cheryl B. Welch (New York: Cambridge University Press, 2006), 1.

15 Welch, "Tocqueville," 1.

16 Welch, "Tocqueville," 1.

17 Tocqueville, *Democracy in America*, 485.

18 Tocqueville, *Democracy in America*, 426.

19 Mélonio, *Tocqueville*, 337.

SECTION 3
IMPACT

THE FIRST RESPONSES

KEY POINTS

- Tocqueville's critics argued that a monarchy was preferable to a democracy* in France.
- France was making the transition to democracy when *Democracy in America* was published in 1835. This may have influenced the generally favorable reception it received.
- Tocqueville did not change his views in the light of criticisms of the book.

Criticism

Alexis de Tocqueville's *Democracy in America* was an extraordinary success and was hailed as a masterpiece at the time. But it attracted criticism nevertheless.[1]

A reviewer in the conservative magazine *Gazette de France** decried America's racial record and argued that a true monarchy would be preferable to an American presidency. The review also suggested that France could imitate the United States government only when it had no more wars to fight and no dangerous neighbors or citizens who disrespected its laws.[2]

Another conservative reviewer criticized American democracy because it overturned the principle of hierarchy, something considered sacred by conservative commentators.[3] Reviewers associated with the legitimist movement in France—which argued that the right of the Bourbon* dynasty to rule should be upheld—were also critical of Tocqueville's views on religion in the United States.[4]

It is probable that these criticisms were based on the reviewers'

❝ When he read the 1835 volumes, Royer-Collard, one of Tocqueville's intellectual mentors, wrote, 'since Montesquieu there has been nothing like *Democracy in America.* **❞**

Isaac Kramnick,* introduction to *Democracy in America*

ideological differences with Tocqueville. In 1830 the idea of a democratic revolution had erupted in France. Parisian students and workers had called for such a republic but the middle class had successfully insisted on retaining a constitutional monarchy.[5] It is possible that the reviewers who criticized aspects of Tocqueville's work were monarchists themselves and thus may have been likely to criticize the idea of France becoming a democratic republic. Tocqueville was also attacked by the historian and Doctrinaire* François Guizot* and the writer Edouard Alletz,* men opposed both to democracy and to the American model of government.[6]

Both Tocqueville's critics and his peers, then, were similarly motivated by ideological differences.

Responses

The first volume of *Democracy in America* was published in 1835 and the second in 1840. Although criticisms were made after the first volume, Tocqueville did not include a new foreword and did not choose not to respond to the critics when the second volume was published—perhaps because the generally accepted view was that this was a fine work. Major Parisian journals and many provincial newspapers agreed that *Democracy in America* was a masterpiece.[7]

It is also possible that the views of Tocqueville's critics had become increasingly marginalized and unpopular by the time the second volume of *Democracy in America* was published.[8] After the revolution of 1848*—only eight years after Volume Two had been published—the

French king Louis-Philippe* abdicated the throne and fled to England and votes for all men had been introduced.[9] Support for the monarchy was already, perhaps, considered a minority view by 1840, and so Tocqueville's critics would not have been particularly influential. Tocqueville may have simply decided that their criticisms did not deserve a response.

Conflict And Consensus

Tocqueville's political actions would also suggest he rejected his critics' views. He was elected to the lower chamber of the French Parliament, the Chamber of Deputies,* in 1839. Having condemned slavery in *Democracy in America*, Tocqueville publicly labeled it a moral abomination and called for slavery to be abolished in the French colonies*.[10] After the abdication of King Louis-Philippe in 1848, Tocqueville was elected to a committee charged with drafting a new French constitution*.[11] Perhaps reflecting his fear of centralized power, Tocqueville proposed a system of checks and balances on absolute power.[12] His later work, *The Ancien Régime and the Revolution*, also addressed the issue of centralized power, which he had previously discussed in *Democracy in America*. Always consistent, Tocqueville's political actions suggest that his critics did not influence his thinking in any substantial way.

Tocqueville's critics held anti-democratic views that would seem archaic to modern readers. This goes a long way to explain why these critics have had so little influence, and why *Democracy in America* is still seen as a success and a classic work of political science.

NOTES

1   Alexis de Tocqueville, *Democracy in America* (London: Penguin, 2003), xxiii.

2   Hugh Brogan, *Alexis de Tocqueville: Prophet of Democracy in the Age of Revolution* (London: Profile Books, 2010), 292.

3   Brogan, *Alexis de Tocqueville*, 292.

4   Brogan, *Alexis de Tocqueville*, 292.

5   Tocqueville, *Democracy in America*, xv–xvi.

6   Françoise Mélonio, *Tocqueville and the French* (Charlottesville: University of Virginia Press, 1998), 34.

7   Brogan, *Tocqueville,* 294.

8   Brogan, *Tocqueville*, 292.

9   Tocqueville, *Democracy in America*, xxxviii–xxxix.

10 Tocqueville, *Democracy in America*, xxxvii–xxxviii.

11 Tocqueville, *Democracy in America*, xxxix.

12 Tocqueville, *Democracy in America*, xxxix.

MODULE 10
THE EVOLVING DEBATE

KEY POINTS

- Alexis de Tocqueville's ideas about the tyranny of the majority* moved the consensus from the idea that democracy* risked anarchy* towards the idea that it could, in fact, lead to a stifling conformity.

- There is a school of thought inspired by Tocqueville's views about civil society* and its benefits.

- Political scientists today seek to measure the link between civil society and democracy.

Uses And Problems

Alexis de Tocqueville's idea of the tyranny of the majority influenced the thinking of the nineteenth century British philosopher and economist John Stuart Mill,* a great admirer of Tocqueville's work. In his autobiography, Mill wrote that after reading Tocqueville his own thoughts "moved more and more in the same channel."[1] In his review of the first volume of *Democracy in America*, Mill wrote: "There should exist somewhere a great social support for opinions and sentiments different from those of the mass."[2] Mill argued that the need to protect minority views would become increasingly important as the power of the majority grew.[3]

In a later essay, *On Liberty*, published in 1859, Mill again returned to the idea of the tyranny of the majority, echoing the ideas of Tocqueville by arguing that there was a need to safeguard against the "tyranny of prevailing opinion and feeling."[4] Mill said that this tyranny was a consequence of an egalitarian society. As society became more equal, the middle class began to participate more in the social and

> **❝** A collateral subject on which also I derived
> great benefit from the study of Tocqueville was the
> fundamental question of centralization. **❞**

Richard Hunter, *Plato's Symposium*

political life of the state. The problem, according to Mill, was assimilation. "Formerly, different ranks, different neighbourhoods, different trades and professions, lived in what might be called different worlds; at present to a great degree in the same ... And the assimilation is still proceeding."[5]

Like Tocqueville, Mill believed that public opinion dominated politics. He argued that "individuals are lost in the crowd. In politics it is almost a triviality to say that public opinion now rules the world."[6]

The idea of the tyranny of the majority was a game-changer in the political thought of the era. When Tocqueville wrote *Democracy in America* the generally held belief was that democracy would lead to anarchy.[7] But the concept of tyranny of the majority—as expressed by Tocqueville and later by Mill—suggested the real risk of democracy was not anarchy, but conformity.

Schools Of Thought

In *Democracy in America*, Tocqueville praises America's civic engagement, writing: "In Europe, governments often bewail the absence of this community spirit, for everyone agrees that it is an ingredient in public order and tranquility."[8] Tocqueville argues that civic engagement is important for democracy to function, claiming that the "life of township is constantly brought to people's notice and makes its presence felt through the fulfillment of a duty or by the exercise of a right. Such a political fact keeps society in a state of continuous yet calm activity which animates it without disturbing it."[9]

Echoes of this idea are found in the neo-Tocquevillian school of thought (the school of thought founded on Tocqueville's writings and beliefs). These academics, recognizably inspired by Tocqueville, believe that belonging to associations has a positive impact on how people relate to each other. Their argument is that associations help to foster the social trust and mutual help that is necessary for a healthy democracy.[10] According to neo-Tocquevillians, a vibrant civil society* is an important building block of society. Likewise, a diminished civil society is a cause for concern.[11]

One thinker who is consistently associated with the neo-Tocquevillian school of thought is the American political scientist Robert Putnam.* Putnam is the author of two of the most-cited social science publications of the latter half of the twentieth century: *Making Democracy Work*, published in 1993, and *Bowling Alone*, published first as an essay in 1995 and then expanded into book form and published in 2000.[12] Putnam's work focuses on the value of social capital* (roughly, the connections between individuals). He agreed with Tocqueville's belief that American civil associations contributed to democracy, writing that these associations "contribute to the effectiveness and stability of democratic government."[13] He takes this view because "associations instill in their members habits of cooperation, solidarity, and public-spiritedness."[14] Putnam also claims that "a dense network of secondary associations both embodies and contributes to effective social collaboration."[15]

In Current Scholarship

Putnam has modernized the ideas of Alexis de Tocqueville by testing them. In his 1993 book *Making Democracy Work*, Putnam measured the success of 20 Italian regional governments. Amongst other factors, Putnam looked at the extent to which each government was located in a community that participated actively in public affairs.[16] His conclusion—with other factors being constant—was that a high level of civic participation was clearly connected with good governance and a successful democracy.[17]

He went on to test the benefits of civic engagement more broadly. Rather than simply focusing on the link between civic engagement and democracy, he investigated whether links exist between civic engagement and other matters of importance to society. In his bestselling book *Bowling Alone*, Putnam argued that links exist between high levels of civic engagement and better outcomes in areas such as health, education, and the economy.

The neo-Tocquevillian argument that civil society benefits democracy has been adopted by other academics, among them the University of Leicester's Professor Laura Morales* and the University of Twente's Dr Peter Geurts.* These researchers have suggested that associations are "schools of democracy," arguing that they generate positive attitudes towards other social and political institutions.[18]

NOTES

1   Terence H. Qualter, "John Stuart Mill, Disciple of Tocqueville," *Political Research Quarterly* 13, no. 4 (1960): 884.

2   Qualter, "John Stuart Mill, Disciple of Tocqueville," 886.

3   Qualter, "John Stuart Mill, Disciple of Tocqueville," 886.

4   Qualter, "John Stuart Mill, Disciple of Tocqueville," 883.

5   Qualter, "John Stuart Mill, Disciple of Tocqueville," 884.

6   Qualter, "John Stuart Mill, Disciple of Tocqueville," 886.

7   Alexis de Tocqueville, *Democracy in America* (London: Penguin, 2003), xxv.

8   Tocqueville, *Democracy in America*, 80.

9   Tocqueville, *Democracy in America*, 81.

10 Sheri Berman, "Civil Society and Political Institutionalization," *American Behavioral Scientist* 40, no. 5 (1997).

11 Berman, "Civil Society and Political Institutionalization."

12 Harvard University Department of Government, "Robert Putnam,"
    Department of Government, Harvard University, accessed June 7, 2013,
    http://www.gov.harvard.edu/people/faculty/robert-putnam.

13 Robert D. Putnam et al., *Making Democracy Work: Civic Traditions in
    Modern Italy* (Princeton: Princeton University Press, 1993), 89.

14 Putnam, Leonardi, and Nanetti, *Making Democracy Work*, 90.

15 Putnam, Leonardi, and Nanetti, *Making Democracy Work*, 90.

16 Putnam, Leonardi, and Nanetti, *Making Democracy Work*, 86–89.

17 Putnam, Leonardi, and Nanetti, *Making Democracy Work*, 115.

18 Laura Morales and Peter Geurt, "Associational Involvement," in *Citizenship
    and Involvement in European Democracies: A Comparative Analysis*, ed.
    Jan W. Van Deth, José Ramón Montero, and Anders Westholm (New York:
    Routledge, 2007), 135.

MODULE 11
IMPACT AND INFLUENCE TODAY

KEY POINTS

- Some of the views expressed in *Democracy in America* are still used in debates about the welfare state* and civil society.*

- *Democracy in America* can be interpreted as saying that a government that takes care of all its citizens' needs discourages those citizens from thinking for themselves. Critics argue that comprehensive government welfare programs have a role to play in a democracy.

- Tocqueville suggests that strong civic associations help to underpin a healthy democracy—but critics say that some associations may actually harm democracy.

Position

In *Democracy in America,* Alexis de Tocqueville expresses ideas that are still used in contemporary debates. One of these debates concerns the role that government should play in ensuring the welfare of its citizens. Without necessarily citing de Tocqueville, conservatives in the United States use his fear of "democratic despotism"* (a term describing a powerful centralized state that saps individual resourcefulness) as an argument against a welfare state.[1]

Another debate focuses on the extent to which a strong civil society is necessary in a democracy. *Democracy in America* has inspired the neo-Tocquevillian* school of thought, according to which the vibrancy of civil society is an important indicator of the health of a democracy.[2] Tocqueville believed that membership of civic associations helped a democracy to function well. Certain academics, including the

> **"** We want to talk about civic participation that weakens liberal democracy. We want to talk about bad civil society. **"**
>
> Simone Chambers and Jeffrey Kopstein, *Bad Civil Society*

American political scientists Robert Putnam* and Theda Skocpol,* agree, citing Tocqueville's views in support of their own belief that a vibrant civil society is good for democracy.

Other academics, however, dispute the extent to which associations can create an effective democracy.[3] These include the University of Toronto's Simone Chambers* and Jeffrey Kopstein,* who argue that the benefits of civil society are too readily assumed and that civil society actually has the potential to harm democracy. Associations can form that only admit a certain type of person, for example, and this can promote intolerance.

Interaction

The Austrian-born American sociologist Peter L. Berger* and the American cleric and writer Richard John Neuhaus* are in favor of a reduced role for the state when it comes to welfare. They believe that communities can solve their own problems and a government that supplies welfare services may undermine community initiative.[4] They also believe community organizations act as a buffer against excessive government intervention.[5] This is a view that goes back to Tocqueville, who believed that community organizations are an essential part of democratic life.[6] His opinion was that such organizations keep democracies healthy because they are all about citizens acting for themselves, rather than being directed to act by the state.

Berger and Neuhaus's view challenges those, such as the Scottish academics Alex Law,* Gerry Mooney,* and William Maloney* and the English scholars Graham Smith* and Gerry Stoker,* who take the view that the state, rather than its citizens, should have the main responsibility for the well-being of society.[7]

Democracy in America has also been used by thinkers such as Robert Putnam to argue that civil associations "contribute to the effectiveness and stability of democratic government."[8] Putnam takes this view because "associations instill in their members habits of cooperation, solidarity, and public-spiritedness."[9] Other academics argue that certain associations may in fact promote intolerance and inequality, say by being too inward-looking, thereby undermining democracy.[10]

The Continuing Debate

Tocqueville's ideas have inspired some to say that, when it comes to welfare, community effort can be a substitute for large-scale government intervention. Theorists such as the American academic Steven Rathgeb Smith* and the American political scientist Michael Lipsky* dispute this. They argue that while initiatives such as food banks and soup kitchens do help to feed the hungry, they cannot replace a widespread government policy such as food stamps* (vouchers exchangeable for food.)[11] These authors are not engaged in a debate with Alexis de Tocqueville, but they are debating how his ideas are used by those who favor a reduced welfare state.

Tocqueville's work also inspired the idea that civil society is beneficial. Academics such as Simone Chambers* and Jeffrey Kopstein* respond to this by arguing that it cannot be taken for granted that involvement in associations will *automatically* benefit democracy.[12] They argue that this involvement may not always be a good thing. Chambers and Kopstein have coined the term "bad civil society" to describe the dark side of associations, arguing that racist and xenophobic* societies might spread hatred and undermine political structures, rather than enhancing democracy.[13]

As with Rathgeb Smith and Lipsky, these authors are not primarily concerned with Tocqueville's ideas as voiced in *Democracy in America*. Instead they are disputing how Tocqueville's ideas have been taken on by thinkers such as Robert Putnam.[14]

NOTES

1 See Alexis de Tocqueville, *Democracy in America* (London: Penguin, 2003), 606, and Caleb Crain, "Tocqueville for the Neocons," *New York Times*, January 14, 2001.

2 Sheri Berman, "Civil Society and Political Institutionalization," *American Behavioral Scientist* 40, no. 5 (1997): 564.

3 Cheryl B. Welch, "Tocqueville in the Twenty-First Century," in *The Cambridge Companion to de Tocqueville*, ed. Cheryl B. Welch (New York: Cambridge University Press, 2006), 1, 4.

4 Steven Rathgeb Smith and Michael Lipsky, *Nonprofits for Hire: The Welfare State in the Age of Contracting* (Cambridge, MA: Harvard University Press, 2009), 26.

5 Smith and Lipsky, *Nonprofits for Hire*, 26.

6 Smith and Lipsky, *Nonprofits for Hire*, 26

7 Alex Law and Gerry Mooney, "The Maladies of Social Capital II: Resisting Neo-liberal Conformism," *Critique* 34, no. 3 (2006): 260; W. Maloney, G. Smith, and G. Stoker, "Social Capital and Urban Governance: Adding a More Contextualized 'Top-Down' Perspective," *Political Studies* 48, no. 4 (2000).

8 Robert D. Putnam, Robert Leonardi, and Raffaella Y. Nanetti, *Making Democracy Work: Civic Traditions in Modern Italy* (Princeton: Princeton University Press, 1993), 89.

9 Putnam, Leonardi, and Nanetti, *Making Democracy Work*, 90.

10 Simone Chambers and Jeffrey Kopstein, "Bad Civil Society," *Political Theory* 29, no. 6 (2001): 839–40.

11 Smith and Lipsky, *Nonprofits for Hire*, 26–27.

12 Chambers and Kopstein, "Civil Society," 838.

13 Chambers and Kopstein, "Civil Society," 839–40.

14 Chambers and Kopstein, "Civil Society," 842.

MODULE 12
WHERE NEXT?

KEY POINTS

- Tocqueville's ideas about democratic despotism* continue to influence debates about government intervention. This trend looks set to continue.

- The work done by the American political scientist Robert Putnam* on the importance of associational involvement has ensured that Tocqueville's ideas about civil society remain relevant.

- Tocqueville's text sets out a program for a stable, prosperous and free democracy.

Potential

Alexis de Tocqueville covered an extraordinary range of topics in *Democracy in America*. The text's depth continues to draw readers, particularly in America, where some academics, among them the historian Isaac Kramnick,* argue that Tocqueville's observations are still relevant to the nation today.[1]

It is certainly true that Tocqueville's ideas continue to shape political thought in America. His description of democratic despotism—the institution of an all-powerful centralized state that would reduce individual citizens to the status of sheep, shepherded along by the government without questioning its decisions—has shaped opinion on both sides of the political spectrum in the United States.

Different political thinkers, however, interpret the meaning of the phrase differently. For conservatives, Tocqueville's democratic despotism is an argument against a welfare state.[2] For liberals, however,

> **" America in the 1830s provided Tocqueville with a glimpse of the institutional mechanisms that forestall the immoderations of the democratic soul. "**
> Joshua Mitchell, *The Fragility of Freedom: de Tocqueville on Religion, Democracy and the American Future*

the term seems more relevant to some of the activities carried out by the government during the administration of President George W. Bush* such as the imprisoning of supposed Al-Qaeda* terrorists in Guantánamo Bay* without trial and American citizens being wiretapped without a warrant.[3]

It is very likely that Tocqueville's idea of democratic despotism will continue to be developed as the debate about what the idea actually means goes on.

Future Directions

Tocqueville's ideas about the value of civic society* are likely to be taken further by the American political scientist Robert Putnam.* Putnam's argument about the importance of individual involvement in civic associations has been very influential. For Putnam, these associations generate "social capital"*—they create a network of relationships that allow communities to function effectively. In the United Kingdom, Putnam's book *Bowling Alone* has been used as a resource when compiling government reports. A 2004 Home Office paper, which acclaimed the benefits of community engagement, referred to *Bowling Alone* a number of times. In particular, it noted Putnam's research showing how social capital can have favorable outcomes for health and democracy.[4]

Although *Bowling Alone* was published as a book in 2000, Putnam had introduced many of the ideas it contained in an essay of the same name published in 1995. Bill Clinton,* then the president of the

United States, used Putnam's findings on civic engagement and associational involvement to inspire passages of his 1996 State of the Union address.*[5] The World Bank* has also made use of Putnam's ideas. A report published in 2000 acknowledged that "the seminal research of … Robert Putnam on civic participation and institutional performance … has provided the influence for most of the current work."[6]

Summary

Alexis de Tocqueville's text challenged conventional thinking about democracies. Two of *Democracy in America*'s most enduring themes are the dangers of concentrated, centralized power and the problem of government excess. While other authors of his era speculated that democracies would lead to anarchy,*[7] Tocqueville was concerned about the government exercising too much control over the lives of its citizens.

Democracy in America is still important because Tocqueville's ideas—particularly about government intervention and people's involvement in associations—continue to inform debates about the welfare state* and civil society. The work has also influenced the thinking of major political theorists and scientists. It was especially admired by the British philosopher John Stuart Mill,* a proponent of minimal government control who used the concept of the tyranny of the majority* in his influential essay *On Liberty*.

Meanwhile, Tocqueville's argument that Americans' involvement in associations helped strengthen their democracy has been adopted by the American political scientist Robert Putnam in his books *Bowling Alone* and *Making Democracy Work*. These were two of the most widely cited social science publications of the latter half of the twentieth century.[8]

Finally, Tocqueville's work is also key because it alerts us to the threats and dangers that all democracies can face. By carefully considering what France could learn from the American experience of democracy, Tocqueville came to outline a political program for any democracy that prizes stability, prosperity and liberty.[9]

NOTES

1 Alexis de Tocqueville, *Democracy in America* (London: Penguin, 2003), xii.

2 Tocqueville, *Democracy in America*, 606; Crain, "Tocqueville."

3 Tocqueville, *Democracy in America*, 606; Crain, "Tocqueville."

4 B. Rogers and E. Robinson, "The Benefits of Community Engagement," in *A Review of Evidence*, ed. Home Office Active Citizenship Centre (London: IPPR, 2004), 19, 48.

5 A. Portes, "Social Capital: Its Origins and Applications in Modern Sociology," *Annual Review of Sociology* 24 (1998): 18.

6 Michael Woolcock and Deepa Narayan, "Social Capital: Implications for Development Theory, Research, and Policy," *World Bank Research Observer* 15, no. 2 (2000): 229.

7 Tocqueville, *Democracy in America*, xxv.

8 Harvard University Department of Government, "Robert Putnam," accessed October 11, 2013, http://www.gov.harvard.edu/people/faculty/robert-putnam.

9 James T. Schleifer, *The Chicago Companion to de Tocqueville's Democracy in America* (Chicago: University of Chicago Press, 2012), 1.

GLOSSARY

GLOSSARY OF TERMS

Abdicate: intentionally leave a position of the highest authority or status. If a monarch renounces the throne, they are said to have "abdicated."

Académie Française: An academic body made up of 40 carefully chosen members who are charged with addressing issues relating to the French language.

Al-Qaeda: a militant, global organization that aggressively follows the principles of what is usually termed "Islamism" (a politicized form of the Islamic religion dedicated to the establishment of a global "caliphate"—an Islamic state).

Anarchy: the absence of government or authority, usually understood to be a state of disorder or even chaos.

Aristocracy: families of the highest social class or status in certain societies, typically people of noble birth. Plato, however, defines "aristocracy" as a form of government headed by a true statesman who would act according to what was right and what ought to be done.

Bourbon monarchy: the royal family of France, temporarily restored to the throne between 1814 and 1830 in the aftermath of the French Revolution of 1789.

Cabinet: men and women appointed to advise or to report to a president or a chief minister in a government, frequently heading important governmental departments such as health, transport, or defense.

Chamber of Deputies: the former lower law-making body of the French Parliament, now superseded by the body known as the National Assembly ("Assemblée Nationale").

Charter of 1814: a French constitutional text decreeing limits on the monarch's powers following the restoration of the Bourbon monarchy in 1814.

Civil Society: a network of groups and communities of citizens joined together by common interests and activities.

Constitution: a document describing the obligations and regulations that define the purpose and nature of a nation's government.

Constitutional monarchy: a system of government where the head of state is a monarch whose power is limited by a constitution (the set of principles according to which a state is governed).

Democracy: a system of government where citizens are involved in the process of making decisions that affect them, usually through elected representatives. The Greek philosopher Plato argued that in a democracy people would have the freedom to do anything— including breaking the law.

Despotism: a form of government defined by the concentration of power in a single individual. A "despot" is usually understood to use their power cruelly.

Democratic despotism: A term coined by Alexis de Tocqueville to describe the dangerous potential outcome of a democracy that took care of its citizens' needs to the greatest extent. The citizens in such a democracy with too much centralized power would come to stop thinking for themselves, Tocqueville argued.

Doctrinaires: a group of French Royalists who argued for a form of representative government in France to work in conjunction with the monarchy.

Enlightenment: a movement in seventeenth- and eighteenth-century Europe that challenged commonly held ideas based in tradition and faith, and tried to advance knowledge through rationality and science.

French Revolution: a period of very great political and social upheaval in France that began in 1789 and ended in 1799 with the military leader Napoleon Bonaparte seizing power. The Revolution marked French society very deeply; its political consequences were felt across Europe and the colonized world.

Food stamps: vouchers issued by the state to low-income citizens, which can be exchanged for food.

Gazette de France: first published in 1631, the *Gazette* was the first weekly magazine published in France. In the nineteenth century it became a journal with royalist leanings, supportive of the Bourbon monarchy.

Great Depression: a significant economic downturn experienced by the Western world in the years 1929–39.

Guantánamo Bay: a military prison established by the United States of America at the Guantánamo Bay Naval Base in Cuba in 2002. Its purpose was to hold and interrogate suspected members of the terrorist group Al-Qaeda.

Knickerbocker: a New York-based magazine published between 1833 and 1865.

Monarchy: a state headed by a king or a queen, or the royal family to which that king or queen belongs.

Napoleonic Era: a period in European history from 1799 to 1815 dominated by the 15-year rule of the military and political leader Napoleon Bonaparte.

Neo-Tocquevillian: a school of thought inspired or influenced by the writings of Alexis de Tocqueville.

Oligarchy: a small group of people, generally understood today to be extremely wealthy, who have control over an entire country or organization. "Oligarchy" was defined by the Greek philosopher Plato as "the form of government in which rulers are elected for their wealth."

Parlements: formerly the highest courts of law in France.

Political Theory: a field within the discipline of political science. Political theorists focus on theoretical claims rather than empirical claims about the nature of politics.

Representative government: a form of government defined by the delegation of power to a body of elected leaders; also known as "representative democracy."

Revolution of 1848: the French revolution provoked by a government clampdown on critics of the regime. The people of Paris took to the streets and directed their anger at their king,

Louis-Philippe, who abdicated the throne and fled to England.

Second Republic: the name of the French government of the years between the revolution of 1848 and its president Louis-Napoleon Bonaparte declaring himself Emperor Napoleon III in 1851.

Social capital: an idea popularized by the American political scientist Robert Putnam. It refers to the connections between individuals and the social networks, trust, and reciprocity that those connections involve.

State of the Union address: the annual address of the president of the United States to the American law-making body known as "Congress."

Suffrage: the right to vote in the election of public officials to the law-making bodies of a democratic representative government.

Superpowers: states that have a dominant position in international relations.

Supreme Court: a final court of appeal and final analyst of the Constitution of the United States.

Timocracy: a form of government where those who hold office must own property and where rulers are motivated by honor or ambition. The Greek philosopher Plato defined timocracy as "the government of honor."

Tyranny: a government that rules by cruelty and oppression. The Greek philosopher Plato argued that democracy would result in a chaotic society, and a tyrant would seize power to restore order.

Tyranny of the majority: a term describing the trampling on the fundamental rights of minorities by the majority in a democracy—a form of government that, it has been argued, all-but guarantees majority rule. The tyranny of the majority was a particular concern of political theorists of the eighteenth century.

Ultras: A group of hard-line supporters of royal power in post-revolutionary France who sought to strengthen the position of the monarchy.

Welfare State: a state in which the economic and social well-being of citizens is protected by governmental institutions, usually funded by taxes. It is based on the principles of equality of opportunity, equitable distribution of wealth, and public responsibility.

World Bank: the International Bank for Reconstruction and Development. Known as the "World Bank," it is an organization of 188 countries, based in Washington, DC, that assists low- and middle-income countries to reduce poverty and develop their economies.

Xenophobia: a prejudice against people from another country.

PEOPLE MENTIONED IN THE TEXT

Edouard Alletz (1798–1850) was a French diplomat and writer. He argued against democracy, favoring a constitutional monarchy.

Gustave de Beaumont (1802–66), a magistrate and penal reformer, was Alexis de Tocqueville's traveling companion for the 1831 journey to the United States described in Tocqueville's *Democracy in America*.

Peter L. Berger (b. 1929) is a sociologist who is currently Professor Emeritus of Religion, Sociology and Theology at Boston University. He co-authored *To Empower People: From State to Civil Society* in 1977.

Napoleon Bonaparte (1769–1821) was born in Corsica and rose spectacularly through the French army to become general. In 1799 he overthrew the French Republic in a coup d'état and in 1804 declared himself Emperor Napoleon I. His military and political genius made him master of Europe until his defeat to the British at Waterloo in 1815.

Louis-Napoleon Bonaparte (1808–73) was the nephew and heir of Napoleon Bonaparte. He became president of the French Second Republic in 1848 after the abdication of Louis-Philippe, and then organized a coup d'etat in 1851, declaring himself emperor and taking the title Napoleon III in 1852.

George W. Bush (b. 1946) was president of the United States of America from 2001 to 2009, elected as the candidate of the Republican Party.

Simone Chambers, a professor of political science, is the current director for the Centre for Ethics at the University of Toronto. She argues that associational involvement will not always benefit democracy.

Charles X (1757–1836) was a French monarch who ruled France for the six years between 1824 and 1830 before the revolution that forced him to abdicate the throne.

François-René de Chateaubriand (1768–1848) was a French writer and politician. He supported the monarchy, but wanted to introduce some elements of the parliamentary system.

Bill Clinton (b. 1946) was president of the United States from 1993 to 2001, elected as the candidate of the Democratic Party.

Pierre-Paul Royer-Collard (1763–1845) was a French statesman and philosopher. He was the leader of the Doctrinaires, a group arguing for representative government in France in the early nineteenth century.

Peter Geurts is an associate professor of research methods and statistics at the University of Twente in Holland. He is associated with the neo-Tocquevillian school of thought.

François Guizot (1787–1874) was a French statesman and historian who supported a constitutional monarchy. He was a member of the Doctrinaires, a group arguing for representative government in France in the early nineteenth century.

Georg Wilhelm Friedrich Hegel (1770–1831) was a German philosopher and a major figure in the movement known as "German idealism."

Andrew Jackson (1767–1845) was president of the United States of America from 1829 to 1837. His followers went on to found the modern Democratic Party.

Terry L. Karl is professor of political science at Stanford University. Her work has often focused on transitions to democracy. She is the author of *The Paradox of Plenty: Oil Booms and Petro-States.*

Jeffrey Kopstein is a professor of political science and current director of the Centre for Jewish Studies at the University of Toronto. He argues that associational involvement will not always benefit democracy.

Isaac Kramnick (b. 1938) is the Richard J. Schwartz Professor of Government at Cornell University.

Alex Law is a professor of sociology at Abertay University in Dundee, Scotland. He argues that the state, rather than its citizens, should have primary responsibility for the well-being of society.

Michael Lipsky is a political scientist and former Massachusetts Institute of Technology professor who is currently a Distinguished Senior Fellow at Demos, a public policy institution in Washington DC. He argues that spontaneous community initiatives cannot replace widespread government programs.

Louis-Philippe (1773–1850) was the French monarch from 1830 to 1848, when he abdicated the throne and fled to the United Kingdom.

Louis XVI (1754–93) was a French monarch who reigned between 1774 and 1792. He was executed during the French Revolution.

Louis XVIII (1755–1824) was a French monarch. He ruled France as a constitutional monarch between 1814 and 1824.

William Maloney is a professor of politics at Newcastle University in England. He argues that the state, rather than its citizens, should have primary responsibility for the well-being of society.

John Stuart Mill (1806–73) was a British philosopher and economist concerned with liberty and state control. He is the author of the respected work *On Liberty*.

Montesquieu (1698–1755) is the name by which the French lawyer and philosopher Charles-Louis de Secondat, Baron de La Brède et de Montesquieu, is commonly known. He was a great influence on Tocqueville.

Gerry Mooney is senior lecturer in social policy at the Open University in Britain. He argues that the state, rather than its citizens, should have primary responsibility for the well-being of society.

Laura Morales is a professor at the University of Leicester in England. She is associated with the neo-Tocquevillian school of thought.

Richard John Neuhaus (1936–2009) was a Christian cleric and writer. He co-authored *To Empower People: From State to Civil Society* in 1977.

Blaise Pascal (1623–62) was a French mathematician and philosopher who had a great influence on Tocqueville.

Plato (427–347 B.C.E.) was an Ancient Greek philosopher. He wrote

The Republic, a foundational work of political theory describing the advantages and disadvantages of different systems of government.

Robert Putnam (b. 1941) is an American Public Policy professor at the Harvard Kennedy School. He is best known for his work on social capital.

Jean-Jacque Rousseau (1712–1788) was a Genevan philosopher, famous for his works about liberty and citizenship.

Theda Skocpol (b. 1947) is an American political scientist and sociologist at Harvard University. She has written about Alexis de Tocqueville, associational involvement and democratic participation in the United States.

Graham Smith is a professor of politics at the University of Westminster in London. He argues that the state, rather than its citizens, should have primary responsibility for the well-being of society.

Steven Rathgeb Smith holds the Louis A. Bantle Chair in Business and Government Policy at the Maxwell School of Syracuse University in the United States. He argues that spontaneous community initiatives cannot replace widespread government programs.

Gerry Stoker is a professor of politics and governance at the University of Southampton in England. He argues that the state, rather than its citizens, should have primary responsibility for the well-being of society.

Voltaire (1694–1778) is the name by which François-Marie Arouet is commonly known. A French philosopher of the Enlightenment, Voltaire argued in favor of separation between church and the state.

WORKS CITED

WORKS CITED

Allen, Michael P. "Hegel Between Non-Domination and Expressive Freedom Capabilities, Perspectives, Democracy." *Philosophy and Social Criticism* 32, no. 4 (2006): 493–512.

Altman, David and Rossana Castiglioni, "Democratic Quality and Human Development in Latin America: 1972–2001," *Canadian Journal of Political Science* 42, no. 2 (2009).

Barker, Ernest. *The Political Thought of Plato and Aristotle*. Chelmsford: Courier Corporation, 2012.

Berger, Peter L. and Richard John Neuhaus. *To Empower People: From State to Civil Society*. Washington: American Enterprise Institute Press, 1977.

Berman, Sheri. "Civil Society and Political Institutionalization." *American Behavioral Scientist* 40, no. 5 (1997).

Bernstein, Richard J. *The Restructuring of Social and Political Theory*. Philadelphia: University of Pennsylvania Press, 1978.

Brogan, Hugh. *Alexis de Tocqueville: Prophet of Democracy in the Age of Revolution.* London: Profile Books, 2010.

Brooks, Thom. "Plato, Hegel, and Democracy." *Bulletin of the Hegel Society of Great Britain* 53, no. 54 (2006): 24–50.

Carrithers, David W. "Montesquieu and Tocqueville as Philosophical Historians." In *Montisquieu and His Legacy*. Edited by Rebecca Kingston. New York: State University Press of New York, Albany 2009.

Chambers, Simone, and Jeffrey Kopstein. "Bad Civil Society." *Political Theory* 29, no. 6 (2001): 837–65.

Crain, Caleb. "Tocqueville for the Neocons." *New York Times*, January 14, 2001.

Craiutu, Aurelian. "Between Scylla and Charybdis: The 'Strange' Liberalism of the French Doctrinaires." *History of European Ideas* 24, nos. 4–5 (1998): 243–65.

— — —. "Tocqueville and the Political Thought of the French Doctrinaires (Guizot, Royer-Collard, Rémusat)." *History of Political Thought* 20, no. 3 (1999): 456–93.

Gershman, Sally. "Alexis de Tocqueville and Slavery." *French Historical Studies* 9, no. 3 (1976): 467–83.

Harvard University Department of Government, "Robert Putnam." Department of Government, Harvard University. Accessed October 11, 2013, http://www.gov. harvard.edu/people/faculty/robert-putnam.Held, David. *Political Theory and the*

Modern State. London: Wiley, 2013.

Helme, G. and Steven Levitsky. "Informal Institutions and Comparative Politics." *Perspectives on Politics* 2, no. 4 (2004): 725–40.

Jennings, Jeremy. "Revolution and the Republic." *A History of Political Thought in France since the Eighteenth Century*. Oxford: Oxford University Press, 2011.

Karl, Terry Lynn. "Economic Inequality and Democratic Instability." *Journal of Democracy* 11, no. 1 (2000): 149–50.

Kaufman, Robert R. "The Political Effects of Inequality in Latin America: Some Inconvenient Facts," *Comparative Politics* 41, no. 3 (2009).

Koritansky, John C. "Decentralization and Civic Virtue in Tocqueville's 'New Science of Politics.'" *Publius* 5, no. 3 (1975): 63–81.

Kramnik, Isaac. Introduction to *Democracy in America*, by Alexis de Tocqueville. London: Penguin, 2003.

Law, Alex and Gerry Mooney. "The Maladies of Social Capital II: Resisting Neo-liberal Conformism." *Critique* 34, no. 3 (2006): 260.

Lawler, Peter Augustine. *The Restless Mind: Alexis de Tocqueville on the Origin and Perpetuation of Human Liberty*. Lanham: Rowman & Littlefield, 1993.

Lijphart, Arend. "Comparative Politics and the Comparative Method." *The American Political Science Review* 65, no. 3 (1971): 682–93.

Lowrey, Annie. "Income Inequality May Take Toll on Growth." *New York Times*, October 16, 2012.

Maloney, William, Graham Smith, and Gerry Stoker. "Social Capital and Urban Governance: Adding a More Contextualized 'Top-Down' Perspective." *Political Studies* 48, no. 4 (2000).

Mélonio, Françoise. "Tocqueville and the French." In *The Cambridge Companion to de Tocqueville*. Edited by Cheryl B. Welch. New York: Cambridge University Press, 2006.

———. *Tocqueville and the French*. Charlottesville: University of Virginia Press, 1998.

Mill, John Stuart. *Autobiography*. London: Penguin Classics, 1990.

Mitchell, Joshua. *The Fragility of Freedom: de Tocqueville on Religion, Democracy and the American Future*. Chicago: University of Chicago Press, 1995.

Morales, Laura and Peter Geurt, "Associational Involvement." In *Citizenship and Involvement in European Democracies: A Comparative Analysis*. Edited by Jan W. Van Deth, José Ramón Montero, and Anders Westholm. New York: Routledge, 2007.

Neuhaus, Richard John and Peter L. Berger. *To Empower People: From State to Civil Society*. Washington: American Enterprise Institute Press, 1977.

Newton, Kenneth, and Jan W. van Deth. *Foundations of Comparative Politics*. Cambridge: Cambridge University Press, 2009.

Plato: *The Republic*. Translated by Tom Griffith. Edited by G. R. F. Ferrari. Cambridge: Cambridge University Press, 2000.

Portes, A. "Social Capital: Its Origins and Applications in Modern Sociology." *Annual Review of Sociology* 24 (1998): 18.

Putnam, Robert D. *Bowling Alone: The Collapse and Revival of American Community*. New York: Simon & Schuster, 2000.

— — —. Robert Leonardi, and Raffaella Y. Nanetti, *Making Democracy Work: Civic Traditions in Modern Italy.* Princeton: Princeton University Press, 1993.

Qualter, Terence H. "John Stuart Mill, Disciple of Tocqueville." *Political Research Quarterly* 13, no. 4 (1960): 884.

Rathgeb Smith, Steven, and Michael Lipsky. *Nonprofits for Hire: The Welfare State in the Age of Contracting*. Cambridge, MA: Harvard University Press, 2009.

Rogers, B. and E. Robinson. "The Benefits of Community Engagement." In *A Review of Evidence*. Edited by Home Office Active Citizenship Centre. London: IPPR, 2004.

Schleifer, James T. *The Chicago Companion to de Tocqueville's Democracy in America*. Chicago: University of Chicago Press, 2012.

Tocqueville, Alexis de. *Democracy in America.* Translated by Gerald Bevan. London: Penguin, 2003.

— — —. *Democracy in America*. Translated by Henry Reeve. Washington: Regnery Publishing, 2003.

— — —. *Writings on Empire and Slavery*. Translated and edited by Jennifer Pitts. Baltimore: J. H. U. Press, 2001.

— — —. *The Ancien Régime and the Revolution.* Translated by Gerald Bevan. London: Penguin, 2008.

Welch, Cheryl B. " Tocqueville in the Twenty-First Century." In *The Cambridge Companion to de Tocqueville*. Edited by Cheryl B. Welch. New York: Cambridge University Press, 2006.

Woolcock, Michael and Deepa Narayan. "Social Capital: Implications for Development Theory, Research, and Policy." *World Bank Research Observer* 15, no. 2 (2000): 229.

THE MACAT LIBRARY
BY DISCIPLINE

AFRICANA STUDIES

Chinua Achebe's *An Image of Africa: Racism in Conrad's Heart of Darkness*
W. E. B. Du Bois's *The Souls of Black Folk*
Zora Neale Huston's *Characteristics of Negro Expression*
Martin Luther King Jr's *Why We Can't Wait*
Toni Morrison's *Playing in the Dark: Whiteness in the American Literary Imagination*

ANTHROPOLOGY

Arjun Appadurai's *Modernity at Large: Cultural Dimensions of Globalisation*
Philippe Ariès's *Centuries of Childhood*
Franz Boas's *Race, Language and Culture*
Kim Chan & Renée Mauborgne's *Blue Ocean Strategy*
Jared Diamond's *Guns, Germs & Steel: the Fate of Human Societies*
Jared Diamond's *Collapse: How Societies Choose to Fail or Survive*
E. E. Evans-Pritchard's *Witchcraft, Oracles and Magic Among the Azande*
James Ferguson's *The Anti-Politics Machine*
Clifford Geertz's *The Interpretation of Cultures*
David Graeber's *Debt: the First 5000 Years*
Karen Ho's *Liquidated: An Ethnography of Wall Street*
Geert Hofstede's *Culture's Consequences: Comparing Values, Behaviors, Institutes and Organizations across Nations*
Claude Lévi-Strauss's *Structural Anthropology*
Jay Macleod's *Ain't No Makin' It: Aspirations and Attainment in a Low-Income Neighborhood*
Saba Mahmood's *The Politics of Piety: The Islamic Revival and the Feminist Subject*
Marcel Mauss's *The Gift*

BUSINESS

Jean Lave & Etienne Wenger's *Situated Learning*
Theodore Levitt's *Marketing Myopia*
Burton G. Malkiel's *A Random Walk Down Wall Street*
Douglas McGregor's *The Human Side of Enterprise*
Michael Porter's *Competitive Strategy: Creating and Sustaining Superior Performance*
John Kotter's *Leading Change*
C. K. Prahalad & Gary Hamel's *The Core Competence of the Corporation*

CRIMINOLOGY

Michelle Alexander's *The New Jim Crow: Mass Incarceration in the Age of Colorblindness*
Michael R. Gottfredson & Travis Hirschi's *A General Theory of Crime*
Richard Herrnstein & Charles A. Murray's *The Bell Curve: Intelligence and Class Structure in American Life*
Elizabeth Loftus's *Eyewitness Testimony*
Jay Macleod's *Ain't No Makin' It: Aspirations and Attainment in a Low-Income Neighborhood*
Philip Zimbardo's *The Lucifer Effect*

ECONOMICS

Janet Abu-Lughod's *Before European Hegemony*
Ha-Joon Chang's *Kicking Away the Ladder*
David Brion Davis's *The Problem of Slavery in the Age of Revolution*
Milton Friedman's *The Role of Monetary Policy*
Milton Friedman's *Capitalism and Freedom*
David Graeber's *Debt: the First 5000 Years*
Friedrich Hayek's *The Road to Serfdom*
Karen Ho's *Liquidated: An Ethnography of Wall Street*

The Macat Library By Discipline

John Maynard Keynes's *The General Theory of Employment, Interest and Money*
Charles P. Kindleberger's *Manias, Panics and Crashes*
Robert Lucas's *Why Doesn't Capital Flow from Rich to Poor Countries?*
Burton G. Malkiel's *A Random Walk Down Wall Street*
Thomas Robert Malthus's *An Essay on the Principle of Population*
Karl Marx's *Capital*
Thomas Piketty's *Capital in the Twenty-First Century*
Amartya Sen's *Development as Freedom*
Adam Smith's *The Wealth of Nations*
Nassim Nicholas Taleb's *The Black Swan: The Impact of the Highly Improbable*
Amos Tversky's & Daniel Kahneman's *Judgment under Uncertainty: Heuristics and Biases*
Mahbub Ul Haq's *Reflections on Human Development*
Max Weber's *The Protestant Ethic and the Spirit of Capitalism*

FEMINISM AND GENDER STUDIES

Judith Butler's *Gender Trouble*
Simone De Beauvoir's *The Second Sex*
Michel Foucault's *History of Sexuality*
Betty Friedan's *The Feminine Mystique*
Saba Mahmood's *The Politics of Piety: The Islamic Revival and the Feminist Subject*
Joan Wallach Scott's *Gender and the Politics of History*
Mary Wollstonecraft's *A Vindication of the Rights of Women*
Virginia Woolf's *A Room of One's Own*

GEOGRAPHY

The Brundtland Report's *Our Common Future*
Rachel Carson's *Silent Spring*
Charles Darwin's *On the Origin of Species*
James Ferguson's *The Anti-Politics Machine*
Jane Jacobs's *The Death and Life of Great American Cities*
James Lovelock's *Gaia: A New Look at Life on Earth*
Amartya Sen's *Development as Freedom*
Mathis Wackernagel & William Rees's *Our Ecological Footprint*

HISTORY

Janet Abu-Lughod's *Before European Hegemony*
Benedict Anderson's *Imagined Communities*
Bernard Bailyn's *The Ideological Origins of the American Revolution*
Hanna Batatu's *The Old Social Classes And The Revolutionary Movements Of Iraq*
Christopher Browning's *Ordinary Men: Reserve Police Batallion 101 and the Final Solution in Poland*
Edmund Burke's *Reflections on the Revolution in France*
William Cronon's *Nature's Metropolis: Chicago And The Great West*
Alfred W. Crosby's *The Columbian Exchange*
Hamid Dabashi's *Iran: A People Interrupted*
David Brion Davis's *The Problem of Slavery in the Age of Revolution*
Nathalie Zemon Davis's *The Return of Martin Guerre*
Jared Diamond's *Guns, Germs & Steel: the Fate of Human Societies*
Frank Dikotter's *Mao's Great Famine*
John W Dower's *War Without Mercy: Race And Power In The Pacific War*
W. E. B. Du Bois's *The Souls of Black Folk*
Richard J. Evans's *In Defence of History*
Lucien Febvre's *The Problem of Unbelief in the 16th Century*
Sheila Fitzpatrick's *Everyday Stalinism*

Eric Foner's *Reconstruction: America's Unfinished Revolution, 1863-1877*
Michel Foucault's *Discipline and Punish*
Michel Foucault's *History of Sexuality*
Francis Fukuyama's *The End of History and the Last Man*
John Lewis Gaddis's *We Now Know: Rethinking Cold War History*
Ernest Gellner's *Nations and Nationalism*
Eugene Genovese's *Roll, Jordan, Roll: The World the Slaves Made*
Carlo Ginzburg's *The Night Battles*
Daniel Goldhagen's *Hitler's Willing Executioners*
Jack Goldstone's *Revolution and Rebellion in the Early Modern World*
Antonio Gramsci's *The Prison Notebooks*
Alexander Hamilton, John Jay & James Madison's *The Federalist Papers*
Christopher Hill's *The World Turned Upside Down*
Carole Hillenbrand's *The Crusades: Islamic Perspectives*
Thomas Hobbes's *Leviathan*
Eric Hobsbawm's *The Age Of Revolution*
John A. Hobson's *Imperialism: A Study*
Albert Hourani's *History of the Arab Peoples*
Samuel P. Huntington's *The Clash of Civilizations and the Remaking of World Order*
C. L. R. James's *The Black Jacobins*
Tony Judt's *Postwar: A History of Europe Since 1945*
Ernst Kantorowicz's *The King's Two Bodies: A Study in Medieval Political Theology*
Paul Kennedy's *The Rise and Fall of the Great Powers*
Ian Kershaw's *The "Hitler Myth": Image and Reality in the Third Reich*
John Maynard Keynes's *The General Theory of Employment, Interest and Money*
Charles P. Kindleberger's *Manias, Panics and Crashes*
Martin Luther King Jr's *Why We Can't Wait*
Henry Kissinger's *World Order: Reflections on the Character of Nations and the Course of History*
Thomas Kuhn's *The Structure of Scientific Revolutions*
Georges Lefebvre's *The Coming of the French Revolution*
John Locke's *Two Treatises of Government*
Niccolò Machiavelli's *The Prince*
Thomas Robert Malthus's *An Essay on the Principle of Population*
Mahmood Mamdani's *Citizen and Subject: Contemporary Africa And The Legacy Of Late Colonialism*
Karl Marx's *Capital*
Stanley Milgram's *Obedience to Authority*
John Stuart Mill's *On Liberty*
Thomas Paine's *Common Sense*
Thomas Paine's *Rights of Man*
Geoffrey Parker's *Global Crisis: War, Climate Change and Catastrophe in the Seventeenth Century*
Jonathan Riley-Smith's *The First Crusade and the Idea of Crusading*
Jean-Jacques Rousseau's *The Social Contract*
Joan Wallach Scott's *Gender and the Politics of History*
Theda Skocpol's *States and Social Revolutions*
Adam Smith's *The Wealth of Nations*
Timothy Snyder's *Bloodlands: Europe Between Hitler and Stalin*
Sun Tzu's *The Art of War*
Keith Thomas's *Religion and the Decline of Magic*
Thucydides's *The History of the Peloponnesian War*
Frederick Jackson Turner's *The Significance of the Frontier in American History*
Odd Arne Westad's *The Global Cold War: Third World Interventions And The Making Of Our Times*

The Macat Library By Discipline

LITERATURE

Chinua Achebe's *An Image of Africa: Racism in Conrad's Heart of Darkness*
Roland Barthes's *Mythologies*
Homi K. Bhabha's *The Location of Culture*
Judith Butler's *Gender Trouble*
Simone De Beauvoir's *The Second Sex*
Ferdinand De Saussure's *Course in General Linguistics*
T. S. Eliot's *The Sacred Wood: Essays on Poetry and Criticism*
Zora Neale Huston's *Characteristics of Negro Expression*
Toni Morrison's *Playing in the Dark: Whiteness in the American Literary Imagination*
Edward Said's *Orientalism*
Gayatri Chakravorty Spivak's *Can the Subaltern Speak?*
Mary Wollstonecraft's *A Vindication of the Rights of Women*
Virginia Woolf's *A Room of One's Own*

PHILOSOPHY

Elizabeth Anscombe's *Modern Moral Philosophy*
Hannah Arendt's *The Human Condition*
Aristotle's *Metaphysics*
Aristotle's *Nicomachean Ethics*
Edmund Gettier's *Is Justified True Belief Knowledge?*
Georg Wilhelm Friedrich Hegel's *Phenomenology of Spirit*
David Hume's *Dialogues Concerning Natural Religion*
David Hume's *The Enquiry for Human Understanding*
Immanuel Kant's *Religion within the Boundaries of Mere Reason*
Immanuel Kant's *Critique of Pure Reason*
Søren Kierkegaard's *The Sickness Unto Death*
Søren Kierkegaard's *Fear and Trembling*
C. S. Lewis's *The Abolition of Man*
Alasdair MacIntyre's *After Virtue*
Marcus Aurelius's *Meditations*
Friedrich Nietzsche's *On the Genealogy of Morality*
Friedrich Nietzsche's *Beyond Good and Evil*
Plato's *Republic*
Plato's *Symposium*
Jean-Jacques Rousseau's *The Social Contract*
Gilbert Ryle's *The Concept of Mind*
Baruch Spinoza's *Ethics*
Sun Tzu's *The Art of War*
Ludwig Wittgenstein's *Philosophical Investigations*

POLITICS

Benedict Anderson's *Imagined Communities*
Aristotle's *Politics*
Bernard Bailyn's *The Ideological Origins of the American Revolution*
Edmund Burke's *Reflections on the Revolution in France*
John C. Calhoun's *A Disquisition on Government*
Ha-Joon Chang's *Kicking Away the Ladder*
Hamid Dabashi's *Iran: A People Interrupted*
Hamid Dabashi's *Theology of Discontent: The Ideological Foundation of the Islamic Revolution in Iran*
Robert Dahl's *Democracy and its Critics*
Robert Dahl's *Who Governs?*
David Brion Davis's *The Problem of Slavery in the Age of Revolution*

Alexis De Tocqueville's *Democracy in America*
James Ferguson's *The Anti-Politics Machine*
Frank Dikötter's *Mao's Great Famine*
Sheila Fitzpatrick's *Everyday Stalinism*
Eric Foner's *Reconstruction: America's Unfinished Revolution, 1863-1877*
Milton Friedman's *Capitalism and Freedom*
Francis Fukuyama's *The End of History and the Last Man*
John Lewis Gaddis's *We Now Know: Rethinking Cold War History*
Ernest Gellner's *Nations and Nationalism*
David Graeber's *Debt: the First 5000 Years*
Antonio Gramsci's *The Prison Notebooks*
Alexander Hamilton, John Jay & James Madison's *The Federalist Papers*
Friedrich Hayek's *The Road to Serfdom*
Christopher Hill's *The World Turned Upside Down*
Thomas Hobbes's *Leviathan*
John A. Hobson's *Imperialism: A Study*
Samuel P. Huntington's *The Clash of Civilizations and the Remaking of World Order*
Tony Judt's *Postwar: A History of Europe Since 1945*
David C. Kang's *China Rising: Peace, Power and Order in East Asia*
Paul Kennedy's *The Rise and Fall of Great Powers*
Robert Keohane's *After Hegemony*
Martin Luther King Jr.'s *Why We Can't Wait*
Henry Kissinger's *World Order: Reflections on the Character of Nations and the Course of History*
John Locke's *Two Treatises of Government*
Niccolò Machiavelli's *The Prince*
Thomas Robert Malthus's *An Essay on the Principle of Population*
Mahmood Mamdani's *Citizen and Subject: Contemporary Africa And The Legacy Of
Late Colonialism*
Karl Marx's *Capital*
John Stuart Mill's *On Liberty*
John Stuart Mill's *Utilitarianism*
Hans Morgenthau's *Politics Among Nations*
Thomas Paine's *Common Sense*
Thomas Paine's *Rights of Man*
Thomas Piketty's *Capital in the Twenty-First Century*
Robert D. Putman's *Bowling Alone*
John Rawls's *Theory of Justice*
Jean-Jacques Rousseau's *The Social Contract*
Theda Skocpol's *States and Social Revolutions*
Adam Smith's *The Wealth of Nations*
Sun Tzu's *The Art of War*
Henry David Thoreau's *Civil Disobedience*
Thucydides's *The History of the Peloponnesian War*
Kenneth Waltz's *Theory of International Politics*
Max Weber's *Politics as a Vocation*
Odd Arne Westad's *The Global Cold War: Third World Interventions And The Making Of Our Times*

POSTCOLONIAL STUDIES

Roland Barthes's *Mythologies*
Frantz Fanon's *Black Skin, White Masks*
Homi K. Bhabha's *The Location of Culture*
Gustavo Gutiérrez's *A Theology of Liberation*
Edward Said's *Orientalism*
Gayatri Chakravorty Spivak's *Can the Subaltern Speak?*

PSYCHOLOGY

Gordon Allport's *The Nature of Prejudice*
Alan Baddeley & Graham Hitch's *Aggression: A Social Learning Analysis*
Albert Bandura's *Aggression: A Social Learning Analysis*
Leon Festinger's *A Theory of Cognitive Dissonance*
Sigmund Freud's *The Interpretation of Dreams*
Betty Friedan's *The Feminine Mystique*
Michael R. Gottfredson & Travis Hirschi's *A General Theory of Crime*
Eric Hoffer's *The True Believer: Thoughts on the Nature of Mass Movements*
William James's *Principles of Psychology*
Elizabeth Loftus's *Eyewitness Testimony*
A. H. Maslow's *A Theory of Human Motivation*
Stanley Milgram's *Obedience to Authority*
Steven Pinker's *The Better Angels of Our Nature*
Oliver Sacks's *The Man Who Mistook His Wife For a Hat*
Richard Thaler & Cass Sunstein's *Nudge: Improving Decisions About Health, Wealth and Happiness*
Amos Tversky's *Judgment under Uncertainty: Heuristics and Biases*
Philip Zimbardo's *The Lucifer Effect*

SCIENCE

Rachel Carson's *Silent Spring*
William Cronon's *Nature's Metropolis: Chicago And The Great West*
Alfred W. Crosby's *The Columbian Exchange*
Charles Darwin's *On the Origin of Species*
Richard Dawkin's *The Selfish Gene*
Thomas Kuhn's *The Structure of Scientific Revolutions*
Geoffrey Parker's *Global Crisis: War, Climate Change and Catastrophe in the Seventeenth Century*
Mathis Wackernagel & William Rees's *Our Ecological Footprint*

SOCIOLOGY

Michelle Alexander's *The New Jim Crow: Mass Incarceration in the Age of Colorblindness*
Gordon Allport's *The Nature of Prejudice*
Albert Bandura's *Aggression: A Social Learning Analysis*
Hanna Batatu's *The Old Social Classes And The Revolutionary Movements Of Iraq*
Ha-Joon Chang's *Kicking Away the Ladder*
W. E. B. Du Bois's *The Souls of Black Folk*
Émile Durkheim's *On Suicide*
Frantz Fanon's *Black Skin, White Masks*
Frantz Fanon's *The Wretched of the Earth*
Eric Foner's *Reconstruction: America's Unfinished Revolution, 1863-1877*
Eugene Genovese's *Roll, Jordan, Roll: The World the Slaves Made*
Jack Goldstone's *Revolution and Rebellion in the Early Modern World*
Antonio Gramsci's *The Prison Notebooks*
Richard Herrnstein & Charles A Murray's *The Bell Curve: Intelligence and Class Structure in American Life*
Eric Hoffer's *The True Believer: Thoughts on the Nature of Mass Movements*
Jane Jacobs's *The Death and Life of Great American Cities*
Robert Lucas's *Why Doesn't Capital Flow from Rich to Poor Countries?*
Jay Macleod's *Ain't No Makin' It: Aspirations and Attainment in a Low Income Neighborhood*
Elaine May's *Homeward Bound: American Families in the Cold War Era*
Douglas McGregor's *The Human Side of Enterprise*
C. Wright Mills's *The Sociological Imagination*

Thomas Piketty's *Capital in the Twenty-First Century*
Robert D. Putman's *Bowling Alone*
David Riesman's *The Lonely Crowd: A Study of the Changing American Character*
Edward Said's *Orientalism*
Joan Wallach Scott's *Gender and the Politics of History*
Theda Skocpol's *States and Social Revolutions*
Max Weber's *The Protestant Ethic and the Spirit of Capitalism*

THEOLOGY

Augustine's *Confessions*
Benedict's *Rule of St Benedict*
Gustavo Gutiérrez's *A Theology of Liberation*
Carole Hillenbrand's *The Crusades: Islamic Perspectives*
David Hume's *Dialogues Concerning Natural Religion*
Immanuel Kant's *Religion within the Boundaries of Mere Reason*
Ernst Kantorowicz's *The King's Two Bodies: A Study in Medieval Political Theology*
Søren Kierkegaard's *The Sickness Unto Death*
C. S. Lewis's *The Abolition of Man*
Saba Mahmood's *The Politics of Piety: The Islamic Revival and the Feminist Subject*
Baruch Spinoza's *Ethics*
Keith Thomas's *Religion and the Decline of Magic*

COMING SOON

Chris Argyris's *The Individual and the Organisation*
Seyla Benhabib's *The Rights of Others*
Walter Benjamin's *The Work Of Art in the Age of Mechanical Reproduction*
John Berger's *Ways of Seeing*
Pierre Bourdieu's *Outline of a Theory of Practice*
Mary Douglas's *Purity and Danger*
Roland Dworkin's *Taking Rights Seriously*
James G. March's *Exploration and Exploitation in Organisational Learning*
Ikujiro Nonaka's *A Dynamic Theory of Organizational Knowledge Creation*
Griselda Pollock's *Vision and Difference*
Amartya Sen's *Inequality Re-Examined*
Susan Sontag's *On Photography*
Yasser Tabbaa's *The Transformation of Islamic Art*
Ludwig von Mises's *Theory of Money and Credit*

The Macat Library By Discipline

Printed in the United States
by Baker & Taylor Publisher Services